THE OUTBACK WRANGLER

Chopper pilot and dangerous animal expert Matt Wright has spent his life in the great outdoors drawn to creatures that most of us would run away from. He has spent time as an outback musterer (horse wrangler), oil rig worker, soldier in the Australian Army, crocodile egg collector and chopper pilot. Matt's passions and unique skill set have turned into a career as a wildlife re-locator; tracking down, capturing and transporting a diverse range of dangerous animals. His objective is the preservation of wildlife: to remove and relocate problem animals rather than kill.

Matt works in the junction between the world of the wild and the world of humans. As a chopper pilot he is able to access areas that would otherwise be impossible to reach; as a conservationist he brings a unique perspective based on hands-on experience and genuine compassion. Matt's motto is: any animal, anywhere, any time.

THE
OUTBACK
WRANGLER

TRUE TALES OF CROCS, CHOPPERS AND SHOCKERS

MATT WRIGHT

with Tom Trumble

MICHAEL JOSEPH
an imprint of
PENGUIN BOOKS

MICHAEL JOSEPH

UK | USA | Canada | Ireland | Australia
India | New Zealand | South Africa | China

Penguin Books is part of the Penguin Random House group of companies
whose addresses can be found at global.penguinrandomhouse.com.

Penguin
Random House
Australia

First published by Penguin Random House Australia Pty Ltd, 2016

10 9 8 7 6 5 4 3 2 1

Cover design by Adam Laszczuk © Penguin Random House Australia Pty Ltd
Front cover art photographed by Dan Walkington (National Geographic Australia),
designed by Gavin Barnett (National Geographic Australia)
All internal photographs courtesy Matt Wright unless otherwise credited
Text design by Samantha Jayaweera © Penguin Random House Australia Pty Ltd
Typeset in Sabon by Samantha Jayaweera, Penguin Random House Australia Pty Ltd
Colour separation by Splitting Image Colour Studio, Clayton, Victoria
Printed and bound in Australia by Griffin Press, an accredited ISO AS/NZS
14001 Environmental Management Systems printer.

National Library of Australia Cataloguing-in-Publication data:

Wright, Matt, author.
The outback wrangler / Matt Wright, Tom Trumble.
9780143797104 (paperback)

Wright, Matt.
Wildlife conservationists–Australia–Biography.
Air pilots—Australia–Biography.
Television personalities—Australia–Biography.
Australia, Northern–History.

Other Creators/Contributors: Trumble, Tom, author.

591.092

penguin.com.au

CONTENTS

INTRODUCTION

People often ask me how I ended up doing what I do today. It's a reasonable question, given I don't exactly have a normal job. In addition to relocating problem crocodiles, collecting croc eggs and flying choppers, I have an interest in eight businesses, manage a tourist operation west of Darwin and have a show on National Geographic called *Outback Wrangler*.

When I look back on my life, it's easy enough to make sense of it all. I can join the dots and form a picture of how I got here. Not that I had a clue how things would turn out when I was in the middle of it all. There was no path conveniently laid out before me. I had to find my own way.

I'm not saying I didn't have mentors. When I think about some of the people who have come into my life, I count myself lucky. Without their guidance, there is no doubt that things would have turned out differently for me. But I believe the direction our lives take ultimately boils down to individual choices. Nobody else can carry you to the place you want to go. You have to get there yourself.

The choices I've made have not always been good ones. Before the days of *Outback Wrangler*, I was barrelling along a path of reckless stupidity and self-destruction. One more bad decision would have left my future very uncertain. It's no exaggeration to say that I nearly ended up in jail. But I pulled my head in, pursued my passions, learnt from my mistakes and developed an appetite for hard work.

This book begins with my earliest memories as a four-year-old child stranded in Papua New Guinea and finishes up with the first season of *Outback Wrangler*. But it's not a biography. I haven't included every boring detail of my life or named every person I've ever met. Instead, I've made a selection of stories that have shaped my life.

There are memorable encounters with saltwater crocodiles, wild boars, feral cattle and water buffalo. There are also tales from my misspent youth and some of my misadventures on drill rigs and on road trains during the time I was trying to figure out what to do with my life. I've also included some of the weirder and more wonderful characters I have met along the way, from eccentric cattlemen to high-profile personalities.

So if you want to know what makes me tick, then turn the page and keep on reading.

1

Escape from PNG

Bloody Errol. He'd done it again.

There we were – my mum Marie, my sister Holly and our British governess Dawn – sitting in the waiting room of the Australian consulate in Port Moresby, in all sorts of trouble. Errol was nowhere to be seen and Mum had her tits in a tangle. Not that you could blame her. She had two kids under the age of six in her care, Dawn was in serious need of medical treatment and we had no way of getting back to Australia. Outside on the streets, gangs of violent youths were up to no good. Errol had got us into the mess and, as usual, he wasn't there to get us out of it.

It wasn't that my stepfather was a bad bloke or meant us harm. In my opinion, he was just off with the fairies, always dreaming up some crazy adventure. Don't get me wrong, Errol's adventures were some of the best. It's just that they were adventures that took us into dangerous places. His latest harebrained idea – the one that got us into this particular predicament – was a desert-island fantasy that only he could dream up. Errol wanted to live off the land in Rabaul, a small township on the northeastern tip of New Britain, an island in Papua New Guinea. Now, I'm all for kids getting outside and getting their knees dirty. I reckon parents are too cautious with their kids these days. But there is a limit. I think that taking a couple of preschoolers into a remote and dangerous part of PNG for an indefinite period is beyond the limit.

Rabaul is a port town that was all but destroyed when a nearby volcano erupted in 1994. We lived there for six months, about a decade before the eruption. Back then it was a minor tourist destination for scuba divers and snorkellers. Tourists were advised to be alert at all times. Not that I was concerned. In fact, I remember it being a great time.

I'll admit I'm pretty hazy on that period. After all, I was only four. When I call up memories of that time, I sometimes wonder if I'm remembering actual events or reimagining what Mum has told me. But some things do remain vivid in my memory. For instance, I recall playing on a beach with local kids outside the hut where we lived with Dawn. One time on that beach, I found a hole with some local kids. The kids backed away, obviously warned off from going near. What I did next shows just how little I knew about the dangers lurking in that part of the world.

I plunged my hands into the hole and started digging out sand. The kids were all looking on in awe. It didn't take me long to work out why. A snake had burrowed out this hole. Instead of running off when I saw the snake's tail, I grabbed hold of it. The other kids scattered as I pulled out a four-foot-long sea snake. I released the snake and it took off across the beach for the safety of the sea. All the kids laughed in amazement. I guess they'd never seen anyone do something like that before. Looking back, I was lucky I wasn't killed. Sea snakes are among the most venomous snakes on the planet.

Mum was in a constant state of worry. Dangerous animals were the least of her concerns. The real danger existed within the community. Now I'm not going to badmouth the people of PNG. They are friendly and warm with a great zest for life. But as with any community, there are some bad eggs. In Rabaul's case, the bad eggs seemed to come from the copra plantations. Young blokes, bored out of their brains after a long day of work and juiced up on betel nut and grog, would stagger into town and terrorise the community. Violent youths weren't the only danger. There was poor sanitation and tropical diseases like malaria, dengue fever and dysentery. If you got sick out there, there was practically nowhere to get medical treatment.

Errol assured Mum that everything would be fine. He had a knack of putting people at ease. But then, practically without warning, he was gone. On a whim he had decided to travel to Taipei and buy a 50-foot Gardner clipper yacht. His plan was to sail the yacht to Rabaul, pick us up and then head off around the world. It was his latest spur-of-the-moment plan. Errol didn't know too much about yachting and now he was proposing to sail us across the seven seas.

Mum protested, of course. But Errol's mind was made up. He said he'd return in a couple of weeks. A month passed and Errol was yet to return. Sure enough, while he was gone, the shit hit the fan.

Dawn cut herself on a coral reef while swimming. If left untreated, the cut would become infected in the tropical conditions. It's a good thing that Mum was always pretty onto things. In her day, she was a brilliant athlete and an excellent bow hunter, and she has always been passionate about the outdoors. She could handle herself in a crisis. Unlike Errol, I thought she was blessed with common sense. The moment Dawn got sick, Mum made her decision. It was time to head back to Australia.

We took a flight from Rabaul to Port Moresby where our passports were being held. We took a cab to the Port Moresby Travelodge where we could buy our tickets. Then things started to unravel. When Mum tried to buy our one-way tickets to Cairns, the person across the counter told us that Dawn's British passport didn't have the re-entry visa she needed to get back into Australia. They wouldn't sell her a plane ticket until she had the appropriate documentation. Mum was told she'd have to sort the problem out with the Australian consulate.

She was fuming. Heading out onto the streets of Port Moresby was the last thing she wanted to do. PNG's capital was on the brink. Gangs of youths were on the rampage. There was widespread looting and violence, with women reportedly being raped. The government had mobilised its military to quell the violence. But the situation was unpredictable. People were advised to stay at home. Mum and Dawn were fit, attractive women in their late 20s. Walking the streets with two young kids and a bunch of violent rapists on the loose is not anyone's idea of a good time.

A cash bribe can sort out most problems in PNG. For the right amount, we probably would have been able to buy Dawn a ticket and sort out the visa issue in Australia. The problem was that Mum only had enough cash for our flights and a couple of days' worth of food and accommodation.

She got on the phone to Australia and rang my grandmother on reverse charges to explain the situation. Grandma said she would arrange for money to be wired into Mum's account. These days you can transfer money in a blink. All you need are your bank details and a phone. It was a different story back in the early 1980s. Transferring money between accounts took days.

The only option was to try and sort out the problem at the Australian consulate.

Mum kept Holly and me close as we jogged there. We made it without hassle, but the consulate staff told us that the visa would take over a week to process. Sitting around in Moresby for an extended period wasn't an option but the staff wouldn't budge.

Mum was doing a good job keeping it together. There she was, sitting in the waiting room of the Australian consulate with her two littlies, a young woman with a nasty injury, no money and facing at least a week in one of the most dangerous cities in the world. She needed Errol. She got John Wayne instead.

'John Wayne' was the name Mum gave to the man who helped us. She never actually learnt his real name. Somehow Mum found out that John Wayne originally hailed from the Central Coast of New South Wales. He had brought his family out to PNG to set up a prawn-fishing business. Although he'd had some success, he decided to send his family home because life in PNG was getting too dangerous. Maybe having kids of his own made him especially concerned for our wellbeing.

My memories of him are vague. I remember this huge bloke with a booming voice swaggering into the consulate. After unsuccessfully trying to sell his catch to consulate staff, he turned towards the four of us. This is how Mum remembers the conversation:

'Excuse me,' he boomed. 'You look like you need help.'

At first, Mum thought he was trying to pick her up. She tried to shake him off, telling him that everything was fine. But he kept pressing.

'Who are you travelling with?'

'Look,' Mum said, sternly. 'We're really not interested in any liaison at all. We're trying to leave this country and we're having a little trouble.'

'What's the trouble?'

'We've got a medical problem here,' Mum said, pointing to Dawn's injury. She then explained the issue with the visa.

'Why don't I take you in to see my doctor?' he said.

'And why would you want to do that?' Mum asked, more suspicious of his intentions than ever.

'He can give you a medical emergency certificate and we'll be able to get you all on board.'

Mum was skeptical. But she was also out of options. The consulate would be closing its doors soon and we'd be back on the streets. So she accepted the offer.

We all bundled into John Wayne's car and he drove us to his doctor. After Dawn was given a medical emergency certificate, John Wayne took us back to the Travelodge. Mum bought four one-way tickets on the earliest flight, which was at 8 p.m. that night. We had a few hours to kill, so John Wayne stuck around and bought us food and drinks. To cap it all off, he drove us to the airport.

Mum was full of gratitude. With everything that had gone wrong, it seemed amazing that someone was prepared to stick their neck out for a group of strangers. Thankfully, he stuck around to the very end. We needed his help to hurdle one final obstacle.

When we got to the terminal gate, we were told that there were only two spots left on the plane. Mum was beside herself. John Wayne took us all aside.

'Right,' he said. 'You're on!'

'No, they're saying we're not,' Mum said. 'There's only enough space for two.'

'Don't worry about it,' he said. 'Just run! Don't look back. Just get on board that plane!'

We waited for the man at the gate to turn his back and then all four of us sprinted past him. It was only a short run to the aircraft, probably 200 metres. Mum handed over our tickets to the hostess waiting at the bottom of the ramp. She was expecting the lady to knock us back. Instead, she smiled and welcomed us aboard.

We scampered up the ramp before security worked out what had happened. But there were no further problems. The plane was almost empty. The guy at the gate was trying to coax a bribe out of us. John Wayne probably knew all along. If we got past that guy, we were home free.

We never met John Wayne again but whenever Mum brings him up, she does so with a big smile. He was a shining light in what was otherwise a pretty horrific ordeal. Despite the massive relief that swept over my mum when we got airborne, internally she was fuming. Errol was about to cop it.

* * *

I don't remember how long it was after we'd returned from PNG that Mum separated from Errol. It can't have been straight away because Errol was stuck in Taipei for a couple more weeks, organising payment for the yacht. When it was finally his, Errol paid for a crew to sail it to Hong Kong. He flew to Cairns via Sydney where he fronted up to Mum.

Mum is a kind and gentle person, but she is also tough. I should know. I was on the receiving end of more than a few hidings growing up. Most of the time, she had good reason for going off. The time she lost it with Errol was no different. She believed he had put our lives at risk. The fact that he was still persisting with this idea of sailing round the world was probably the tipping point for Mum.

In the end, Errol never got to live his dream of sailing the world. The blokes he hired to sail the boat to Cairns ran into a typhoon off the Philippines. A Thai fishing boat had to tow them into a nearby port after the rudder was destroyed. From there, it was freighted to Hong Kong where Errol sold it off at a loss.

Mum decided to keep us in Cairns. We'd been living there for four months before Errol took us off to Rabaul. Returning to Cairns was supposed to be a new beginning. We originally hailed from Second Valley, a sleepy little coastal town on South Australia's Fleurieu Peninsula, 100 kilometres south of Adelaide. My guess is that, for Mum, Cairns had the advantage of being in Australia but away from her previous life in Second Valley.

* * *

With Errol out of the picture, we were now a party of three. We moved into a small two-bedroom unit. My memories of that period are of fun and adventure. I was a five-year-old kid with no worries. I even enjoyed school.

The weather was too warm to enforce a dress code so the kids rocked up to class wearing no shirt and no shoes. The teachers placed an emphasis on being outside and getting to know the native wildlife. That made me king of the kids, particularly during show and tell. While all the other kids brought junk from home, I was dragging any animal I could find into class. I'd go out the back of our place and catch massive spiders, put them in jars and hand them around the classroom. I'd catch non-venomous snakes and walk into the school with them curled around my neck. Some mornings I'd swim in the local lake, catch a big turtle and lug it to school in my bag. The teachers loved it. Having a live specimen in the class was a sure way to keep everyone's attention and a great way for them to teach. We'd learn everything about the animal, from habitat and diet to the animal's predators and prey.

But there was one occasion where I overstepped the mark. By now, spiders, snakes, lizards, turtles and insects were old hat. I needed to step up my game. So I climbed into a tree and bagged myself a fruit bat. I strutted into school, barely able to contain my excitement. *Wait until my mates see this!*

'So,' began the teacher, 'what have you got for us today, Matt?'

The animal had been quiet in my bag. It was a different story when I pulled him out. The bat squawked and carried on, managing to break free from my grasp. My teacher screamed, and with good reason. She was probably terrified of the bat spreading disease.

'Get it out!' she shrieked.

It took about an hour to coax the bloody thing outside with a broom. The bat was so scared it shat everywhere. The smell lingered in the school corridors for over a month. The teachers were not impressed. I was forbidden from bringing bats to school but that was the extent of the punishment. They knew I had made an honest mistake.

When I was not at school, my life was one adventure after another. Mum had joined a bow-hunting club. Every other weekend we'd head out to Fitzroy Island, a picturesque little place located about 30 kilometres off the coast of Cairns. We'd go snorkelling around the island's coral reef or explore the island's rainforest before camping overnight.

Other times we'd head off with a group of Mum's mates to some remote river. While the parents would be off hunting feral pigs, the kids would be floating down the river on tubes, having a ball. If we weren't canoeing or boating, we'd be searching for lizards, pythons, frogs and turtles. At night, someone would tell stories around the campfire as a slaughtered pig was turned on the spit.

One of the members of the club was a French-Canadian by the name of Jerry. He became a sort of father figure to me. I hero-worshipped the bloke. He was fit, muscly, and a skilled hunter. Jerry and I both shared a love of wildlife. He believed that all animals could be approached and handled, no matter how dangerous. During a trip we did on the Great Barrier Reef, he demonstrated this no-fear attitude and deep understanding of animals. We spotted a tiger shark circling the boat and were warned to stay out of the water. Without hesitation Jerry jumped in, swum under the shark and held onto it, gliding peacefully through the water. I was in awe – I wanted to be just like Jerry.

He taught me that the trick with animals is to remain calm, understand their behavior, and stay out of their strike zones. It was Jerry who first tutored me in how to catch venomous snakes, and lucky he did.

Things got a little hairy one night when I was left to my own devices and went exploring. I found what I thought was a python under some outside shelving. I put my wrangling skills to work and began pulling what turned out to be a seven-foot snake, twice my size. It wasn't a python, either. I was holding onto an eastern taipan, one of the deadliest snakes in the world.

I called for help. Mum came barrelling out of the unit. She started screaming the moment she saw the deadly snake dangling perilously close to my body. The snake was getting seriously pissed off, too. I couldn't let it go for fear that it would turn around and nip me. I ran out, away from the unit, and flung the snake as far as I could. Mum came up behind me, took me around the waist and lifted me back inside to lock me up. Lesson learnt.

* * *

Looking back, my guess is that Jerry had a huge thing for Mum. I kind of wished something had developed between the two of them. He had a lot of time for us kids and a lot of knowledge to offer. He exemplified everything I now think a good father should be. He was encouraging, open-minded, and showed me that anything is possible if you put your mind to it.

By this time, Errol had been out of the picture for a while. But Mum and Errol had never got divorced. It turned out that they were talking again, trying to work things out. It was more complicated than just an emotional connection. Mum's professional future was tied up with Errol's. She had been finishing up study in acupuncture and naturopathy. The big plan was for Mum to open up her own clinic with Errol, who was a qualified chiropractor and talented naturopath.

Sure enough, when the school year was up, we packed our bags and returned to where it had all started – South Australia. A kid as young as I was generally accepts the decisions and choices a parent makes. But that didn't mean I was happy about going back.

2

Second Valley Kids

Mum and Errol bought a property in Mount Compass, about an hour's drive south of Adelaide. On the face of it, this was a good place for a kid like me to grow up. There was a lot to keep me entertained – acres of space to roam about and we had horses, chooks, a big fat pig and a hotheaded billy goat. There were also snakes and lizards everywhere.

Moving to Mount Compass meant reconnecting with my old man, who lived with his new family in Second Valley, a drive of 40 minutes from our place. It was strange to see Dad again. Holly and I basically had nothing to do with him the moment Mum and Errol took us up north. Suddenly we were back in each other's lives.

Dad grew up in the foothills of Adelaide, where his family made a living from owning a string of pubs. His parents named him Elliot Bruce Wright, largely because they liked the wordplay after you initialise the first two letters of his name – E. B. Wright, as in 'Eee be right. The joke is lost on most people because Dad has always gone by the name Bruce.

I never met my paternal grandfather. He died from a stroke when Dad was 15, leaving my Nanny Brownie to raise him on her own. Nanny Brownie was an exceptional woman. She was cluey as hell and the second female pilot to get her licence in South Australia, flying Tiger Moths back in the days when you were mad to step into one. She always wanted to fly in the RAAF during the war but was never allowed. She was a local hero and some of her personal belongings are still on display in the Longreach Hall of Fame.

Nanny Brownie kept company with some pretty high-profile names, too. As a lifetime member of the Mount Osmond Golf Club, she played with Sir Donald Bradman and his wife. Sir Donald taught Dad to bowl. He'd put a penny on the middle stump of the wicket and let Dad keep it every time he knocked one off. This must be where Dad developed a love of cricket.

Dad is your classic Aussie bloke: a man who likes to keep things simple. He is a diehard supporter of the Norwood Football Club and Adelaide Crows, loves fishing, cricket and, above all, kicking back with a cold home brew at the end of the day. Dad is practical, resourceful and a good problem-solver. For these reasons, he was Second Valley's go-to person in an emergency. If a fire needed to be put out or people were stuck on the cliffs or someone risked being drowned at sea, everybody knew to call Bruce. His innate ability to get out of sticky situations is something I've inherited.

Dad was a shearer and wool-classer before he retired. He'd work down the southeast coast past Broken Hill, up to the west and then back to his shearing shed in Delamere. After he and Mum got together, they moved to Dad's family holiday house in Second Valley. It was a short-lived relationship. My folks divorced when I was 18 months old, so I don't remember them being together. Following their separation, Mum had full custody of Holly and me. She moved us to Deep Creek, into the pine forest where she broke in horses to support us.

Dad was constantly on the move with travel commitments and, after our move to Deep Creek, we barely saw him. That all changed when we moved back to Second Valley. Holly and I caught up with him every other weekend. Holly would stay with Dad and I'd stay with my mate Jono, whose folks lived two doors down. Although I was under Dad's care, I spent most of the time with Jono, getting up to mischief. But one thing Dad and I did do together was fish.

Both my old man and Jono's dad were fishing mad. They would go fishing together with their mates whenever they had the chance. All of us kids would excitedly go to bed the night before, already in our bathers, and wake at first light to the sound of the tractors pulling the boats down to the water. It seemed like every father in the community would be communicating over radio, getting people organised for the day of fishing. After a quick stop to the general store for 20-cent lollies, an armada of boats would push off from the beach, everyone hoping to catch a big one. Once we were out on the water, we'd troll for squid, then use squid heads to catch snapper and squid tails for whiting. There was never a day we returned without the boat full of fresh fish.

I'll never forget this one particular time when a resident shark began frequenting and circling the bay at Second Valley. The shark had been spotted a number of times and there was a general concern that it would have a crack at the kids who regularly swam off the beach. Locals asked Dad if he could do something about it. Dad had the perfect solution.

He went out in his boat with a couple of sealed 20-litre drums that had been baited up. He anchored the drums and then returned to the shore, parking the boat on the ramp for quick access. For the next three days, Dad sat on the couch watching the cricket while intermittently checking the drums through his binoculars. After a couple of days, Dad saw one of the drums being pulled under. He bolted the door shut, went out in the boat, and brought the shark in. The town was relieved and Dad made sure he ate what he'd killed. Everyone on the street was eating fish and chips for dinner for the next week!

I respected my old man. But even after we returned to South Australia, I didn't really have too much more to do with him. He had remarried and created a new life. Even on those weekends when Mum dropped Holly and me off at his place, I barely saw him. I spent the whole weekend at Jono's house.

Jono and I were like Tom Sawyer and Huckleberry Finn, always looking for another adventure. We'd roam around everywhere, getting up to all sorts of antics. One time we walked the 15 kilometres to Cape Jervis. That was a long way for seven-year-olds and I copped an ear-bashing from Mum when we returned home after dark.

But the real fun was with animals. On a weekend camping trip with Jono's family on the south coast, I decided to bag a couple of dangerous pets. After filling up a bucket with scorpions, we went looking for snakes – it was the perfect place to catch them. That part of Australia is absolutely full of brown snakes.

The eastern brown is the second-most venomous terrestrial snake in the world, the taipan being the most venomous. The bite of a brown snake will bring on diarrhea, vomiting, renal failure and sometimes cardiac arrest. According to the statistics, an adult human has a 20 per cent chance of dying if they are bitten and don't receive medical attention. The odds are worse for the young and the elderly. This is not an animal to be treated lightly.

I'd been warned about brown snakes, but I wasn't the slightest bit concerned. Jerry had said that provided you handle a snake with care and confidence, you have nothing to worry about. I caught three browns on that trip, making sure to stay out of the animal's strike zone, just as Jerry had taught me. They were only small ones – two feet long at most. They were still big enough to give me serious problems if I got bitten, though. I put them in the bucket with the scorpions and draped a towel over the top of them.

Mum came and picked me up on Sunday night and she asked about the bucket. I told her Jono and I had just caught a couple of lizards. I rested the bucket on my lap, having every intention of watching it like a hawk for the two-hour drive back to Mount Compass. I hadn't counted on how tired I was. At some point along the way, I nodded off. Next thing I remember I was looking up at Mum who was gently waking me up.

I sat bolt upright. The bucket was gone! It had fallen onto the floor of the car. I waited for Mum to turn her back before I inspected the bucket. Luckily, it had fallen on its end, trapping the snakes inside. Most of the scorpions escaped in the fall because there were only a couple left. Either that, or the snakes had eaten them.

Mum grabbed the bucket and I was too scared to tell her what was really inside. We walked to my room and mum unknowingly tucked me in with a bucket of brown snakes at the end of my bed. First thing the next morning, I heard an ear-piercing scream. Mum had woken up early to do the weekend's washing. There she was, loading up the washing machine when a juvenile brown snake came up the passage to meet her.

Mum lost her shit. She came running into my bedroom, screaming at me to get out of bed – she knew straight away it had come from my bucket. I was a good sleeper as a youngster. I'd sleep into all hours and it often took a lot to get me out of bed. Mum knew that I wasn't going to move just because a brown snake was scurrying about the house.

She ran back into the laundry and managed to trap one of the snakes in the bucket. But she didn't know there were two more of them roaming free. When I eventually staggered out of bed, the house was in an uproar. Everyone was furious. I got the absolute third degree from Mum on the dangers of brown snakes. I told her to calm down and asked casually if she'd caught the other two. The look on her face was priceless. She couldn't comprehend what she was hearing.

'You better damn well find them before I get home today!'

I had no luck the first day. Fortunately, the snakes didn't make an appearance in front of any patients in the clinic Mum and Errol had set up in the house. I eventually caught one the following morning. It had found its way into the kitchen. It took a couple of weeks for the third snake to turn up. Errol made the discovery. He was sitting on the toilet when he felt something brush past his leg.

'Matt!' he roared. 'Get down here and catch this bloody snake!'

Following this ordeal, Mum and I struck a deal. She would let me keep the snakes in a pit that I dug out the back of our house provided I didn't catch any more. I agreed to the deal and then broke my end of the bargain.

Even at a young age, dangerous animals had a real hold on me. They just fascinated me. I continued catching snakes and adding them to the pit. Mum was none the wiser until she got a call from one of our neighbours. People had seen me lifting up discarded pieces of corrugated iron and dead logs in search of snakes. I caught some big fellas, too – five or six feet long, in some cases.

Mum was terrified that I'd get myself killed. But she knew that no amount of yelling was going to keep me away from snakes. I was drawn to these animals like a magnet. So she tried to broker another deal. If I agreed to stop catching brown snakes, she'd buy me a carpet python when I turned 12. It was a tempting offer – a carpet python is a non-venomous snake that can grow up to 13 feet in length. But I wasn't prepared to wait for three years so I managed to barter her down to my next birthday, which was only a couple of weeks off.

On the morning I turned nine, Mum came into my bedroom and handed me a large shoebox. I opened the lid and pulled out a five-foot beauty. It was the greatest gift I'd ever been given in my life. I named the snake Solomon and kept it as a pet until it died around the time I turned 20.

***

The horses were another highlight on our farm at Mount Compass. My favourite was a big Cleveland Bay thoroughbred named Dolly. She was bred for racing but never made it to the track. Mum got her for a song, but told us not to go near her. She was a powerful and temperamental old mare.

One day, Holly goaded me into taking a ride on her when Mum was out. I was the sort of kid that never knocked back a dare. We saddled her up and on I leapt. It was all going smoothly at first. I walked her around for a bit, feeling completely relaxed. Dolly seemed fine. That was until my sister crept up behind us with a whip and gave the horse an almighty whack across her flanks. Dolly reared up and then bolted. Before Dolly and I disappeared over a hill I caught sight of my sister clutching at her sides in hysterics.

I pulled hard on the reins, but couldn't pull her up. We careered across the paddock, clearing fences and logs. It was all I could do to stay on her back. The horse was fast approaching a road, and out of the corner of my eye I saw a car driving along – fast. We were all on a collision course.

I screamed at the horse to stop, tugging and pulling at the reins as best I could. It made no difference. Seconds from disaster, the driver hit the brake, the car screeching to a halt right in front of us. Dolly was undeterred. She pinned back her ears and leapt over the bonnet. As we landed, I was catapulted out of the stirrups, somehow managing to stay on by grabbing hold of her neck. Dolly galloped around for a few minutes as I pulled myself back on to the saddle. After she calmed down I turned her towards home.

My sister was still falling on the ground in fits of laughter. She thought it was the funniest thing she had ever seen. I didn't ride much for a while after that little episode. I was absolutely filthy at Holly, but I wasn't a tattletale. Holly and I were always at each other growing up, pulling these sorts of stunts. A few months later, I had my revenge.

Next to the old shed on our property was a sheep yard. Errol had electrified the gate to keep Klondyke, our big old family pig, from burrowing out under the fence. Mum didn't like having electric fences with kids running around, so Errol kept it permanently switched off. But he never dismantled the mechanism. It was a simple matter of flicking the switch and – *zap* – back on it went. A brilliant little scheme popped into my head.

The sheep yards were home to a whole lot of our farm animals, including my old billy goat with its big horns. The goat was a real handful, charging anyone who dared to approach. So Errol chained him up to a post in the middle of the yard. Every day, one of us would have to go down and feed him. On the day it was Holly's turn, I leapt into the sheep yard and unchained the goat. Before going to get my sister, I went into the shed and electrified the fence.

'Holly,' I said, doing my best to keep a straight face. 'Errol says you've gotta feed the goat.'

'You do it.'

'Nah. It's your turn.'

Holly let out a sigh, stopped doing whatever she was doing and went to fill up the goat's bowl with water. She wandered down to the yards with the bowl, happily singing to herself and completely oblivious to me stealthily following behind. When she got to the gate, she laid the bowl on the ground and then touched the fence. I reckon I saw her hair stand on end before she launched backwards and started howling. I could barely keep my feet on the ground I was laughing so hard.

Holly turned around towards me and roared. She knew exactly what I had done. Not that she could really complain, not after the stunt she had pulled with the horse. She went into the shed, turned off the electric fence and entered the yard with the bowl. Once she was within 10 metres of the goat, she stopped in her tracks. Something was wrong. The goat was not where it was supposed to be. He was unchained!

For a couple of seconds there was a tense stand-off as the two eyed each other. Holly made the first move. She took a cautious backward step. The goat snorted, leapt up on his back feet and charged. Holly dropped the bowl, screaming. She ran towards the gate, but the goat was onto her in a flash. Holly turned around to meet the attack and managed to grab the animal by his horns. She was running around the yard backwards for at least two minutes, not daring to let go. Somehow, she managed to manoeuvre the goat towards the gate. With all her strength, she pushed him back and then rushed out, slamming the gate in his face. Once she was safe, she flipped me the bird. It was the best entertainment I'd had in a long time.

***

Errol was doing well as a chiropractor but he liked spending money on his boats. His enthusiasm for boating never waned, despite the fiasco with the 50-foot Clipper. He bought a 25-foot Haines Hunter Cat with a pair of 250-horsepower Mercury engines on the back. This was one powerful boat, and he loved any opportunity to take her out.

One Easter, we put the boat on a trailer and took it over to the Yorke Peninsula, a popular holiday destination about three hours from Adelaide. Jono came along for the ride. We launched the boat and headed out to Seal Island, just off Althorpe Island, a craggy rock about 10 kilometres off the coast. It was a beautiful day for boating – barely a breath of wind and the water was dead glassy. Nothing could possibly go wrong. Or so we thought.

To get to Seal Island, you have to cross the Strait. This is a deceptively dangerous stretch of water, full of unseen reefs and submerged sand banks. Even on clear days, you can count on a decent swell rolling across the shallow water. These are waters where even seasoned old salts can get themselves into trouble.

Errol wanted to go diving for crayfish near one of the reefs. I thought it was a bloody stupid idea. That part of the Australian coast is notorious for great white shark attacks. But he wasn't going to be talked out of it. About a mile from Seal Island, Errol drew up alongside a reef. Jono and I were sitting up at the bow of the boat, our legs dangling over the front. I remember looking down and observing the colour of the water change suddenly from dark blue to aqua. The next second, we could clearly see the bottom.

Mum was the first to sound a warning. She started shouting at Jono and me to get back from the bow.

'Look at that!' said Jono, lifting up his arm.

He was pointing at a huge 35-foot wall of water. It was moving fast. Jono leapt to his feet and grabbed hold of the front railing with both hands. I made for the safety of the stern of the boat, but was caught halfway. I managed to grab hold of a handle on the roof of the cabin as the bow dug into the face of the wave. The boat reared upwards the moment it met the wave. I remember going vertical, hanging on tight with one hand as the boat was nearly stood on its end.

Errol had slowed us down. He should have sped up so that we could have pushed over the wave. We slid down the back of the wave and smashed into the reef stern first. I ended up at the bottom of the boat and started sobbing. Jono scrambled back, drenched from head to toe, his eyes as big as saucepans. It was an absolute miracle we didn't capsize, but we weren't out of danger. The wave had pushed us abeam of the oncoming swell, the position of greatest vulnerability in heavy seas. And another massive wave was building.

'Get us the hell out of here!' we all roared at Errol.

Smoke was billowing out of the left engine, which had taken the brunt of the force when the boat was speared backwards into the reef. Luckily, the other engine was still operating. After floundering around on the reef for a few more seconds, Errol gave his remaining engine full throttle. We managed to get away, seconds from disaster.

That was the end of the holiday. Mum was dark on the whole situation. For a while, I thought she was going to call it quits with him again. But it didn't turn out that way.

3

My Mum, the Bow Hunter

Imagine all the pioneering women throughout history who changed the world by breaking boundaries. My mum Marie is like them. She has always challenged convention and stepped out of her expected role to create opportunities for herself and her kids. Her skills as a naturopath are legendary. She has got me through some nasty bugs over the years from Ross River virus to dengue fever.

In many ways, she was ahead of her time. Well before 'organic' and 'super food' became buzzwords, Mum was into eating wholefoods. She spent hundreds of dollars on organic vegetables. God, if only I had known that all the buckwheat and activated food I was being fed would be trendy one day. I could have made an absolute mint!

Not many mums are capable of doing what mine has done. Whether it was ceramics, horse riding, camping, cooking, diving, spearfishing or gardening, Mum has mastered everything she has put her mind to. She approaches life with an open mind, is a great lateral thinker, is a superb problem solver and possesses an uncanny sixth sense.

But of all the things for which Mum is known, bow hunting is probably top of the list. She was the best going round. I'd always hear stories from her friends about her amazing feats with the bow and arrow. The story of her shooting the rabbit is a yarn her friends still talk about to this day. I wasn't actually there but there are photos to prove it.

The story goes that she was out hunting with friends in the dead of night, trying to catch a decent pig for dinner the next day. They weren't having much luck. But there was no shortage of rabbits bouncing about. Mum suggested killing a couple of rabbits for tucker instead. Everyone laughed, and not at the thought of having rabbit. Rabbits are small, fast and will bolt if you get too close. Even at the best of times – in clear weather with good visibility – that makes them very tricky game for a bow hunter. At night, successfully bow hunting a rabbit is nigh on impossible.

Mum's friends didn't even take her suggestion seriously. While they were debating what to do, Mum had drawn her bow and shot an arrow. Everyone turned to follow Mum as she walked towards her target. There, in the middle if the grass was a rabbit on its side with an arrow right up its bum. In near pitch darkness, Mum was able line up her target from over 40 metres and hit it with no worries at all.

Mum's mates loved telling me how good she was with the bow. But I didn't need anyone to tell me she was a gun. I saw it firsthand. I'll never forget the day Holly and I were jetty-jumping in Second Valley. The sun was setting and the beach was empty. Mum had been swimming and got out of the water to go to the car. She came back with her bow in hand and I remember asking her what she was doing.

'Do you two want to have dinner on the beach?' she asked.

Holly and I looked at each other, intrigued. Mum came up next to us on the jetty. She leant over the water, took aim at a big fish darting between the pylons and loosed an arrow. She handed me her bow and jumped into the water, coming up with a huge fish, the arrow speared through its gills. That was pretty cool. We ended up lighting a fire near the water and having the fish on coals for dinner.

Mum was a deadeye dick. She had won a whole bunch of awards and there were trophies hanging on walls and sitting on shelves around the house. But to my mind, she never got an award for her greatest feat of hunting – the day she took down the biggest feral pig I have ever seen.

It happened on a camping trip on Kangaroo Island. I was about 11 years old at the time. As always, Jono came along. Located off the South Australian coast, KI – as the locals call it – is the third-largest island along Australia's coastline. The island is 4500 square kilometres of open woodland, farms and small deserts, rimmed with some of the country's most pristine beaches. The natural barrier of the sea has supported a biodiverse and incredibly fragile ecosystem. Like so much of Australia, the modern world has thrown up some challenges for the native species on the island. Of all the problems, there are none bigger than feral animals.

Feral pigs are a disaster for this country. They are highly adaptable creatures, capable of surviving in searing heat and freezing cold. They can live pretty much anywhere, provided they are within a day's march of water. They aren't fussy eaters, either. They will devour anything, from small mammals and larger newborn mammals to nesting birds and eggs. In the absence of their preferred food, pigs will use their nose to burrow into the ground for plant matter and invertebrates like worms and insects. For this reason, there are parts of Australia, particularly up north, that look like they have been taken to by a backhoe. Wild pigs not only threaten native species, they are a constant headache for farmers. Given that a sow typically delivers a litter of six piglets twice a year, the problem is getting worse and has spread to the islands off the mainland.

Wild pigs are just one of many challenges facing the people and native animals of KI. The island's pest problem is a classic example of how the nuisance of escaped farm animals can quickly escalate to a full-blown catastrophe. Today, cats, goats and deer roam free, threatening the island's rich biodiversity. Back in the late 1980s, pigs were the major problem. It was on this camping trip that I discovered that pigs not only threatened native species, they were also incredibly dangerous to humans.

We were staying on a private property with a couple of other mates, Daryl and Rudy. Daryl was getting into the bow hunting with mum. We all loved it, particularly Mum. For a hunter, there was plenty of game that needed to be culled.

We'd been camping for three days straight. It was the depths of winter and a stiff southerly blew a chill from the Antarctic that kept the mercury low. The weather didn't dampen our spirits. We were having a blast. We hunted pig and goat each day, butchered up our kill and then cooked it over the campfire. It was a throw-back to the good old days up in Cairns. But on the third night, the trip took a turn. The hunters became the hunted.

Daryl suggested we go spotlight hunting. We hooked lights onto our old Range Rover four-wheel drive and drove around in a low gear on the paddock. Jono and I were standing up in the back, manoeuvring the lights around, searching for any signs of pigs. Whenever we saw something we would shout out to Mum and Daryl, who were up in the front of the four-wheel drive. Our beams lit up different animals, but they scampered away too quickly for Mum to get a shot away. After an hour, Daryl pulled the car over.

'The sound of the engine is scaring them off,' Daryl said. 'Time to go on foot.'

I asked Mum if I could take the .22 rifle. She said I could, provided I handled it with care. She made me recite the usual rules: keep the muzzle pointed in a safe direction; be sure of the target and what is beyond it; and keep my finger off the trigger until the target is acquired. Once Mum was satisfied, Jono and I headed down a slope.

'Don't go too far,' Mum said.

I had the rifle cradled across my arms and Jono was holding a high-powered torch. It was a beautiful, clear night. The moon lit up undulating hills crisscrossed with fences marking out paddocks. Barely a breath of wind stirred the leaves of the trees. It was so quiet we had no trouble picking up the telltale squeal and snort of a litter of pigs. I grabbed Jono's arm and we both got down on a knee. Jono panned across the landscape, searching for the source of the sound.

'There they are,' he whispered, playing the beam of light over three pigs burrowing their snouts into the ground about 50 metres away. About 10 metres behind the pigs stood a cow minding her own business. It was a strange sight to see feral animals sidled up so close to a farm animal. Something wasn't right. An alarm bell was ringing, but I didn't heed the warning. That was a big mistake.

I raised the rifle and laid one of the pigs across my sights.
The pig was looking straight at me, transfixed by Jono's torch.
I remember the lessons Mum had taught me: keep my breathing
steady and shoot between heartbeats. The adrenaline must have
been pumping because my shot completely missed. The crack of
the rifle shot sent the pigs scurrying. I swore loudly as I watched
the pigs disappear into the night.

'What's that cow doing?' asked Jono.

The cow had turned to face us and started to run at us.

'That's not a cow!' I said, my mind barely registering what my
eyes were seeing. It was a massive boar and it was charging.

'Shoot it!' Jono shouted.

I brought the rifle up and squeezed the trigger. Although the
boar was moving quickly, the animal's sheer size made it an easy
target. The boar squealed, confirming that the bullet had hit the
target. But the animal's layer of fat and hefty shoulder pads acted
like a bulletproof vest. The shot only succeeded in stirring him
up more. I fired again, aiming for the boar's head. Once again,
the boar squealed. I might as well have been throwing pebbles at
him. The boar had closed to within about 20 metres.

'What do we do now?' Jono shouted.

'Run!'

We both leapt to our feet and turned for the car. Mum and
Daryl had obviously heard the gunshots because the spotlight was
trained on our position. Mum was shouting out to us, asking if
everything was okay.

'We're being chased!' I shouted back.

Neither of us dared look back. But I could hear the heavy
breathing of the animal, hot on our tail.

'Move out of the way!' Mum called out.

I was close enough now to see that Daryl was standing next to Mum and had shot an arrow. We heard another high-pitched squeal but it must have lodged into his shoulder pad, because he wasn't slowing down. Jono and I split apart, opening up the target for Mum. I heard the twang of the bow and the whisper of the arrow as it sliced through the night air, followed by another terrible squeal from the boar.

I threw my head around, expecting the animal to have crumpled to the ground. Instead, he was still charging. Mum was nocking another arrow.

'Keep running!' Mum shouted as we bolted past her.

'Get up here!' Daryl shouted. By this time Daryl was kneeling on the back of the four-wheel drive, with his arms hanging over the side. We both leapt up on to the back tray with Daryl's help. Mum had managed to slip another arrow into the boar. It was a brilliant piece of marksmanship. Mum was hitting her target without a spotter to light the boar up. Not that it made a difference. The boar was enraged. And he was rapidly closing in on her.

Mum turned and legged it for the four-wheel drive. She was only 10 metres from the truck, but the boar wasn't letting up, five metres away and closing. Mum dived through the open back door. The boar took his final steps before launching after her. Mum pulled the door shut just in time. The boar cannoned into the side of the car. Jono and I were standing up alongside Daryl on the back when the boar collided with the car. The force of the collision knocked us off our feet.

'Stay down!' Daryl said to us, worried that if we stood we might topple off.

'Everyone all right?' Mum called out.

Daryl shouted back that we were fine. Jono and I scampered

to the side of the tray to get a look at the boar. It was an incredible sight. This was a proper razorback, a big round keg of fat and muscle with a mane of raised fur running down its back. His tusks had been ground away to nothing, which suggested that we were looking at an old animal. I could see Mum's two arrows poking out of his big shoulder pad, but the extent of the animal's wounds was unclear. The collision with the back door had left the animal dazed. He stood still alongside the truck, his snout occasionally dropping low to the ground. We were all expecting him to keel over any second. In fact, the opposite happened. With each passing moment, he regained strength.

After a couple of minutes, the pig took a few tentative steps. We started to follow him in the car and every time we got close he'd have another crack at the side of the vehicle. It was like he was looking for a way in. He turned around in frustration and started walking away.

'Looks like he's packing it in,' I said.

I could not have been more mistaken. The pig was just warming up. He turned around and charged. He launched into the side of the car, smashing into the back door. The car shuddered with the blow.

Mum quietly opened the door on the other side of the car with her bow and swapped places with Daryl who hopped into the driver's seat. As the pig lugged his massive weight back to get a run up, she slipped another arrow into his side. He bucked and squealed, pivoting around and running back into the side of the car.

Eventually, the pig started to weaken and walked off towards where Jono and I had first seen him. Mum managed to get out of the car and followed quietly in the shadows as we held the light on him; he was making a break for the thick scrub. It was crucial that Mum got a good kill shot in the side of him. She was able to go wide and get herself in front of the 300-kilo animal. Mum propped up behind a massive gum tree and waited until the time was right, then drew her bow and let the last arrow fly with perfect precision. The arrow speared in behind the shoulder blade and with a couple more steps this huge beast finally toppled over. After a few moments, Mum walked over to inspect the animal. She had an arrow at the ready to put him out of his misery. She tentatively nudged the animal with her foot. But he remained motionless. Blood was already pooling from his nose and under the carcass.

When Mum sounded the all clear, Jono and I went to have a look at the big animal. His tusks might have been worn away, but he still had a nasty set of fangs. Jono and I were lucky we didn't trip up when we were running away from him. Had either of us done so, those teeth would have torn us apart. At the very least, he would have broken a few of our bones. That was evident just from looking at the back door of the four-wheel drive. The pig had shattered a window and caved the door in.

Daryl pulled out the camera and told mum to crouch alongside the fallen animal – the hunter and the hunted.

4

Raising Hell

Mum's parenting style was unconventional. She was big into personal responsibility and put a lot of faith in Holly and me to perform tasks that I'm sure some parents would deem unsuitable for children. From a young age we learnt how to shoot a rifle, skin animals, cook meals and drive a car. If we were out camping, Mum made us responsible for everything. We packed the car, set up camp, cut the wood, made the bed, lit the fire and scrubbed the toilets.

Mum taught us every single practical life skill you can think of. I cannot imagine a better role model growing up. The way she approached life and the lessons she taught us still ring in my ears today: feed the dog first, tell the truth, never kill animals without a reason, give to people in need and do your chores before you have fun.

She had no concerns about leaving me to my own devices on the weekends, giving me the time and space to become my own person. I would explore the valleys around home and try out the things she'd taught me. She was committed to raising independent children who would be capable and self-sufficient adults. She gave me the drive, discipline, determination, strong work ethic and ability to survive in this sometimes hard and overbearing world. If you can't tell from what I have just shared, I love her dearly. She has made me who I am today.

But that doesn't mean we didn't have our rocky moments. Raising me was no easy task. I was a bloody nightmare. I got a lot of smacks growing up and deserved every one of them. It was hard to drill a message into me. Looking back, I realise the amazing job Mum did. She was capable of being gentle and encouraging one minute and harsh the next. But she was always fair. She was the mother, the father, the disciplinarian and the friend all rolled into one. The person I have become boils down to the lessons she taught me growing up.

If I did something to piss Mum off – which was often – she wouldn't simply berate me or give me a hiding, she would teach me a lesson in an unforgettable way. There are countless examples to draw on, but none more memorable than when she made me skin a fully grown kangaroo with a pocketknife. I was 11 years old. It was extreme tough love. Not that I'm complaining. It was exactly the punishment I deserved.

It happened a couple of hours before Mum had promised to take me rabbiting. I was playing up. I can't really remember why. I guess I was keen to get started. Mum told me to wait while she fed the farm animals. I'll admit it, I was an impatient little shit. If things weren't happening the way I wanted, I'd lose my cool completely.

'C'mon,' I moaned. 'Let's go! You're dragging arse!'

'Watch your mouth!' she shouted. 'If you keep that up, we won't go at all.'

Most kids would have done as they were told. Besides, it wasn't as if there was nothing else to keep me occupied. But I wasn't like most kids. I took a rifle and headed out on my own.

Mum had taught Holly and me from an early age how to handle firearms. She often took us out hunting. And I couldn't have asked for a better teacher – she was passionate about the sport. Not that she was bloodthirsty or anything. In fact, Mum has more respect for animals than anyone I know, even feral pests. She despises cruelty towards animals and drilled into us the importance of giving an animal a clean, instant death.

I shot a couple of rabbits before coming across a big grey kangaroo. Mum was always big on never killing a native animal whose meat or skin you aren't going to use. Her mantra was simple: never take more than you need. She also insisted that you kill an animal as quickly as possible.

I crouched into a shooting position and waited. The kangaroo was grazing. With his head down, my chances of a kill shot were not good. I had to wait. I edged forward and a twig snapped under my foot. The kangaroo lifted his head and stood up to his full size. He was a big animal, at least six feet tall. With his head up I had an easy shot. I aimed and then fired. The roo was dead before he hit the ground. I was pretty proud of myself. There was no pain or suffering. I'd given him a quick death, just as Mum had always taught me.

I took hold of the kangaroo's leg and started dragging him back home. I could hardly wait to show Mum what I had bagged. But he was far heavier than I'd expected, and I was about five kilometres from home. There was no way I would be able to get him back on my own. I dragged him to the bottom of our paddock and left him there. I was thinking either Mum or Errol could come down in the ute and pick him up. I stepped up my pace. I was chomping at the bit to tell everyone about the big animal I'd just shot.

It was well after dark by the time I got home. Mum came thundering out of the house to meet me. I can't remember seeing her so livid. She took me by the arm and gave me a flogging. When I told her that I needed the car to go pick up a big kangaroo I'd shot, she gave me another few wallops.

'I told you to leave the kangaroos alone,' she said

That was one lesson I don't remember her teaching me. Whether she had warned us off the kangaroos before doesn't really matter. Her 11-year-old son had just gone hunting without her permission. She had every reason to be angry.

I was sent to bed without dinner. I thought the punishment was over. I couldn't have been more mistaken.

Around midnight, Mum burst into my bedroom and flicked on the lights. She was still on the warpath.

'Wake up!' she shouted.

'What's going on?'

'Get out of bed!'

'No,' I said, burying my head under the pillow.

She was obviously ready for this reaction. She pulled the pillow away, ripped off my blanket and then hauled me out of bed. When I tried to resist she gave me a few smacks and shoved a backpack into my arms.

'What are you doing?' I asked.

She told me to open the backpack. It was stuffed with plastic bags. In the front pocket there was a pocketknife.

'You're going to head back out and skin that kangaroo,' she said. 'When you're finished, you're gonna bag up all the meat in

38

those plastic bags and bring it back here.'

I started howling. But Mum wasn't going to fall for that old trick. She led me outside and told me she'd be checking the carcass in the morning to make sure I'd done a proper job.

It was a long night. I walked back over the hills, through the scrub, down into valleys and then over to the bottom of the paddock where I'd left the old roo, with nothing but a torch to guide me. I found him about two hours later. Now the real work was about to begin.

The only way to properly skin and bone out an animal is with a large, sharply pointed knife. Not only will you do a better job, you'll also do it quickly. A pocketknife is not nearly the right tool for the task. Obviously I could only move the knife one way or else the blade would fold back on itself. I knew that if I did a substandard job, Mum would dream up some other punishment. So I got stuck in.

Cutting the hide was tough enough. It must have taken me over an hour to remove it all. But trying to cut through tendons and bone with a pocketknife was horrific. Rigor mortis had set in, which made it a little easier, but I still only had a bloody pocketknife. It took me a couple of hours before I started bagging up the meat.

Dawn was a few hours away and the temperature was dropping. I began to lose feeling in my fingers. I was also absolutely exhausted and feeling pretty sorry for myself. The prospect of a five-kilometre walk lugging bags of meat filled me with dread. So I decided on having a sleep. I lay down on the frozen ground next to the carcass and shut my eyes. The problem was the cold. I needed a blanket, but the only thing on hand was the remains of the roo. I wrapped myself in its hide. It smelt a bit but was warm. Within seconds, I was asleep.

I woke up just after dawn, the whole world covered in frost. I finished up bagging the meat and took everything home. I walked in the back door to Mum who had calmed down by that stage. Nevertheless, she still looked at me sternly.

'Well,' she said, 'hopefully you'll learn from this one.'

As each year passed, her hopes were dashed. I became increasingly wilder. Incidents like shooting the kangaroo proved to be pretty mild compared to the hijinks I got up to in the years to come. It all started to lift off around the time I became a teenager. That was when my attitude collided with puberty and things started to get very interesting.

* * *

I never cared much for school. In fact, I hated just about everything about the place. The schoolyard was divided into two groups – the goths and the jocks. I definitely wasn't the type to get dressed up in black clothing and cover my face in make up. Nor was I the type to go and chase balls around all day.

I was bored out of my mind. School down here was completely different to what I had experienced in Cairns. Up there, it felt like the teachers made an effort to engage the students, encouraging kids to pursue the things that they were passionate about. In this place, I was forced to sit through classes that had absolutely no meaning to me. English, maths, music, history and geography all put me to sleep. My mates and I would wag in the afternoon and head to the local pub for beers. Once we were boozed we'd walk down to the golf club and play a few holes to entertain ourselves. We decided this was better than school any day and it became the norm.

The older I got, the worse things became. At first, the discipline issues were fairly minor – falling asleep on my desk, talking back to the teacher, throwing paper planes and blowing spitballs at other kids. Before long, that stuff began to bore me. I set my sights on stirring up the teachers. Getting kicked out of class was my goal.

My standard move was kicking kids' chairs out from under them. If that didn't do the trick I'd start knocking over tables and throwing chairs around the classroom.

'Get out!' the teacher would roar. 'Go see the headmaster!'

Smiling ear to ear, I'd gather up my things and leave. Sometimes I would flip the bird at the teacher for good measure. Job done. In the end, I was spending more time outside the headmaster's office than in the classroom.

One day I'd really had enough of one of my classes. After answering back a few too many times, I got sent outside. There I set my sights on a fire extinguisher. I unhitched it from the wall and walked back inside the classroom. With one squeeze of the trigger the powder shot out like an erupting volcano. The teacher was covered in white and the room began to fill up with powder. The teacher and the whole class were forced outside because it was so thick you could barely breathe. Knowing that this time I would be in serious shit, I took off running.

A lot of the time, I'd ditch school entirely for the day. Sometimes Jono would wag too, or I'd meet up with him after final bell. We'd look for any way to entertain ourselves. One particular favourite was ripping out 'For Sale' signs staked out the front of properties and using them as sleds. Those shiny metal signs used to skim beautifully down a slope.

Once, while wandering through the hills from Second Valley

to Rapid Bay, we came across a discarded car bonnet. With its distinctively curved shape, the bonnet looked to have belonged to a Volkswagen Beetle. Christ knows what it was doing up there. We didn't really care. All we were thinking about was using it as a sled.

We flipped the bonnet on its top, lined it up for the bottom and jumped inside. There was no need to push off with our hands. The hill was covered in pebbles and rocks. With the sharp curve of the bonnet preventing us from digging into the ground, we absolutely flew down that hill. We got airborne a few times, sailing over small ledges and bouncing over boulders. I remember seeing the tops of trees whistling past. There was no way of getting off. We were going too fast. When we finally came to a stop at the bottom, both of us were covered in grazes. Jono had taken most of the skin off his palms in a hopeless attempt to slow our descent with his hands. Sure, it was dangerous. But like all the stunts we used to pull in those days, nobody got hurt – at least not seriously. The real problem was my habit of getting into fights.

It wasn't that I was a bully. In fact, I tended to pick fights with blokes older and bigger than myself. I was just an absolute hothead. If someone so much as looked at me the wrong way, it would be on. Teacher feedback was that I had an attitude problem. My school reports at the end of each term didn't make for great reading, but it was the references to getting into fights in the schoolyard that had my mum most concerned. She was already getting worried when I started coming home with a bloody nose or missing buttons from my shirt.

Truth was, I wasn't only getting into fights on school grounds. Around Second Valley I acted in a very territorial manner. The way I saw it, Jono and I owned Second Valley. If someone stepped onto our turf, we would let them know all about it. Talking back to teenagers older than us often landed us in trouble, like the time we got into a dust up down near the old yabby hole.

The yabby hole was located under a bridge over an inlet at Second Valley. It was one of our favourite spots. Beautiful big yabbies used to burrow into the soft mud under the bridge. The sewage from the local caravan park would run under the bridge, which kept them fat and healthy. We used to fish them out and take them home and cook them up for dinner. I'm not sure our folks would have eaten them if they'd known what they were chewing on.

We were fiercely protective of the yabby hole. It was our place. If we came onto other kids fishing the yabby hole, there would be trouble. There was one occasion when Jono and I nearly bit off more than we could chew. We came across a group of three boys probably about 16 years old fishing the hole. We were outnumbered and these guys were four years older than us. That's quite a large gap at that age. It didn't matter. Jono and I saw red.

We got over the bridge and started mouthing off. They told us to piss off, so we started hocking up phlegm and sent down a few gobs. That got their attention. They climbed up to the bridge, ready to fight. Jono was a skinny little bloke and I wasn't much bigger – and these guys were twice the size of us. But what we lacked in size we made up for in speed. Just before the fists started flying, I leapt in fast at one bloke and pushed him over the railing. He cartwheeled over the side and landed in the river below.

'Run!' I shouted at Jono.

We sprinted across the bridge and headed into the hills. Those blokes were breathing fire. They helped their mate out of the river and then came after us. We had the home ground advantage and knew every square inch of that terrain. We ran them around our patch, hiding in crevices and leading them along false paths. We crested a hill and turned around to check their progress. They'd fallen well behind. They were still keyed up and determined to knock the shit out of us, though. So, of course, we started hurling rocks and pushing little boulders down on them.

'See you later, suckers!' we shouted down at them, as they scampered clear.

Jono and I laughed all the way home with another great story to tell. We were always getting into scraps like that one. But after a while, roaming the hills of Second Valley became boring. By the time I'd become a teenager, I'd graduated to a whole new level of troublemaker. I was chock full of hormones and energy and I had no place to burn it off. School was no longer just tedious. It had become unbearable. I went looking for new ways to alleviate the dreariness of life in the Valley and found a group of like-minded troublemakers along the way.

At a time when the other kids were thinking about getting into university or TAFE or heading straight into the workforce, we were thinking up ways of getting up to no good. We ran amok purely for the thrill of it. If we weren't trespassing, we'd be hot-wiring cars and going for joy rides. It was reckless, dangerous and unbelievably stupid. I knew exactly what I was doing, but my adolescent mind concluded that if I got busted I would be judged as a minor. It was my way of rationalising my atrocious behavior; a way of convincing myself that I wasn't completely giving up on my future.

Parents of badly behaved kids will often justify their child's waywardness by saying that they fell into a bad crowd. That wasn't the case with me – I *was* the bad crowd. Whether I simply drew like-minded kids into my orbit is hard to say. Some parents certainly saw me as a ringleader and a negative influence and told their kids not to hang out with me. In the end, Jono's parents forbade him from seeing me. After the shit we'd pulled over the years, I was surprised it hadn't happened sooner. The tipping point was a weekend holiday where Jono and I raided the minibar in the room we were staying. We got completely shitfaced and then trashed the room. Naturally, our parents were livid.

It would be easy for me to hide behind excuses. My relationship with my old man was non-existent and I had no respect for Errol. So you could say I lacked a positive male role model. There were also more fault lines appearing in Mum and Errol's marriage. Big blow-ups and shouting matches were a daily occurrence. The truth is, none of those things bothered me. Besides, at some point all kids have to take responsibility for their actions. The way I look at it now, I was a teenager completely bored out of my brains. Breaking laws was my way of feeling alive. But it was always going to end badly.

* * *

By now, I was 16 and old enough to drive a car – legally. Jono and I were still catching up despite being warned not to do so. We arranged to drive down to Cape Jervis for a spot of fishing. It wasn't a very well-thought-out trip. We didn't bring along any food or bait. Our plan hinged on shooting a kangaroo. The best part of the roo would be our lunch and uneaten scraps would serve as bait. Jono had packed his crossbow and I had Mum's.

There are obviously very strict rules about shooting animals. For example, hunting on another person's property without permission is illegal. That meant we had to stay out of sight.

'Why don't we head to that national park?' I asked.

The Deep Creek Conservation Park is about a 15-minute drive from Cape Jervis. Like all national parks in Australia, people – especially minors – are forbidden from hunting animals in Deep Creek. A ranger might take out a dangerous animal. Otherwise, killing creatures in national parks is off limits, which made it all the more appealing to us.

We left our Toyota in the empty car park and headed off along one of the walking tracks with our bows. There were kangaroos and wallabies everywhere. We took a couple of shots, but couldn't get a clear path. The animals were lurking behind trees and shrubs, instinctively aware of the danger we presented. Finally, I spotted one in a small clearing off a walking track. I nocked an arrow and took aim, before quickly aborting. A group of bushwalkers had suddenly appeared. We stashed our bows in some scrub behind a tree and pretended we were hiking. An old bloke barrelled up towards us.

'What do you think you're doing?' he shouted.

'What are you on about?' I said.

'Don't play stupid, kid,' he said. 'We saw you shooting arrows with a bow.'

I continued to play dumb. Things got pretty heated. I nearly punched the old bloke but Jono dragged me away. We waited for them to clear off before returning to the place where we had concealed our bows. But they were gone. While the old bloke had been levelling accusations, one of the other hikers must have snuck out of sight and grabbed our gear. This was not good. Mum's bow was her absolute pride and joy. There was no way I was going home without it.

Jono and I knocked our heads together and came up with a plan. We figured the old man was going to report us to the police and hand over our bows as proof. If we could get the jump on him and report our gear stolen, then the whole thing would become his word against ours. All I can say is that it seemed like a good idea at the time.

I got on the phone to National Parks and Wildlife and reported that someone had broken into my car and taken a crossbow and a hunting bow. The police were informed and I was brought in. In the end, it didn't wash with the coppers. This was a small country town. Everybody knew everybody else. The police were always going to take the word of an old man with an impeccable reputation over a wild teenager who was known to the police.

I ended up going to court. I was found guilty and sentenced to 50 hours' community service. I had to 'fess up to the coppers to get the bow back, but I didn't care. Coming clean to the police was far less daunting than fronting up to Mum.

Unexpectedly, community service turned out to be great fun. I was ordered to take extra classes after school with one of the few teachers I actually respected, Mr Truman. Mr Truman's class wasn't like maths, literature, science or history. In other words, it wasn't 50 minutes of torture. He taught carpentry and metal work, the only class where I actually scored decent grades. Those 50 hours of community service were a breeze. As an added bonus, Mum never found out. She didn't even know that the bow was missing in the weeks leading up to the trial. Her mind was on other problems.

5

Pull Your
Bloody Head In!

Errol and Mum divorced. Their marriage had been on the skids
for a long time, but it still came as a shock when it ended. It got
messy. It wasn't just a case of splitting the house and the assets.
They had to work out how to handle the business. Mum's practice and Errol's practice were heavily entwined. Not only did
they run off the same books, their patient lists overlapped. It was
something that the courts would have to sort out.

It was decided that Errol would stay up at Mount Compass
while Mum, Holly and I rented a small house in McLaren
Vale. Holly went to boarding school, so that left Mum and
me. McLaren Vale is a region renowned for producing some of
Australia's finest wine. In this part of the country, the hills are
crisscrossed with vineyards as far as the eye can see. There are
wineries absolutely everywhere.

It wasn't an easy time for Mum. Having an out-of-control
teenager on her hands was absolutely the last thing she needed.
I'm not proud of this period of my life. I was behaving like an
absolute prick at a time when she needed my support. The hours

wasted in court and performing community service after being busted hunting in a national park might have knocked me into line had Mum found out. But she hadn't. It was like I'd gotten away with it. Like a lot of kids in their mid- to late teens, I thought I was bulletproof. My behaviour got worse and worse. Until one time, I went too far.

The incident happened at the start of my last year at school, when the temperature in the classroom was at its hottest. It wasn't even lunchtime, but the day was dragging. So four of us decided to take the afternoon off. A few of the boys had brought their bikes to school. Those of us without bikes were dinked as we went exploring.

I suggested we take a look inside one of the enormous buildings at a local winery. After busting the lock on the door, we all filed in. Inside were these huge metal vats that reached up towards the roof, at least two or three storeys high. At the base of each was a large tap. Crates of empty bottles lined the walls of the storehouse. No second guesses for what happened next.

We had no problems turning the taps on. The challenge was trying to get the wine into the bottle. The mouth of the tap was big enough to fit your fist inside. It was like turning on a fire hydrant. Wine surged out of the tap, ending up all over the floor. For every bottle we filled, probably 200 litres of high-quality wine was wasted. And the four of us went through a lot of bottles.

We sampled the wine from each vat and were all pissed in no time. But it wasn't until we found the sparkling wine that the situation started to get seriously out of control. It was sweeter and more refreshing in the blistering heat. A couple of the boys were chugging entire bottles of the stuff in one go. I was 15 and had hit the grog a few times before. But this was a whole new level of drunkenness. I was completely blind.

Before we left, we must have filled up about 30 bottles to take home. We corked them up and stashed them in our bags. In a half-hearted show at responsibility, I went round and turned off all the taps. By then, the damage was done. Every square inch of floor was covered in wine.

Getting home was a circus. It was challenging enough for those guys who were riding the bikes. For those of us being dinked it was a bloody nightmare. I lost count of the times I fell on the ground. A ride that normally takes about 10 minutes took five times that. We made it to the outskirts of McLaren Vale and started riding through front lawns, knocking down letterboxes and destroying fences. All the way we were laughing uproariously in between hurling insults at bystanders for no particular reason. It was the most amount of fun I'd had in years.

Once we'd made it to the main street, we got even more raucous. People spilled onto the street from the shops to check out who was responsible for the racket. We finally made it back to my place. Luckily, Mum wasn't home. Unluckily, my sister was. The moment I staggered into the house she got straight on the phone.

'Mum,' she yelled into the receiver. 'Matt and the boys are pissed.'

Mum came home and found me halfway down the drive. I did my best to play it straight, but I had no hope. I was completely legless. If I was the most pissed of all of us, then my mate Luke was a close second. At the sight of my Mum bounding up the driveway, he panicked.

'Righto,' he said, trying to get back on his bike. 'I'm off home.'

He got up some speed on the bike and rode straight into the

side of the house. He stumbled to his feet, picked up the bike and had another go. He only made it a few metres before Mum raced over and pulled him off the bike. She frogmarched him towards the house.

'All of you!' she roared. 'Get inside! Now!'

I went straight to my bedroom and started throwing my guts up while Mum called the parents of the other boys. I could hear everyone else spewing up in the front yard while they waited to be collected. Mum brought me a jug of water. It was one of the few things I remember about the night, other than Holly coming into my bedroom and pinching one of the bottles of wine in my bag. That didn't impress me one bit, particularly seeing as she had ratted on me. But I was too hammered to do anything about it.

The following morning, nursing the first serious hangover of my life, Mum took me down to the cop shop. She had been on the phone to the police the previous day. The local copper was a good guy. He knew I'd been in trouble with the law. He also knew that putting me through the courts was not what I needed. The cop rang up the winery and somehow smoothed things over with them. No charges were going to be laid.

Not that I knew any of this at the time. Mum, who was white hot with rage, left me in the waiting room on my own. I was sat in the same room as hardened criminals and rough-looking characters. After about 30 minutes, the sergeant called me in. He sat me down in the interrogation room and told me what was going to happen. His words were that much more power-ful because he was measured when he said them. I was no longer a kid copping a lecture from a parent or a teacher. I was being spoken to like an adult. The implication was clear – I couldn't hide behind being a child anymore.

He pulled out a file of information on me and listed all the things that I'd been convicted of doing in the past. He also mentioned the stuff that I was suspected of doing – shit I thought *nobody* knew about. Then he said that if the winery pressed charges, I'd probably have a record. That would be a permanent stain on my life that would make finding work after school very hard. If I was convicted of another crime, I faced juvenile detention. If I continued breaking the law, I'd most likely end up in jail.

The sergeant talked about what going to jail actually meant – the violence, the rape, all of it. Then he stood up, told me he'd be in touch. There was none of the usual, 'Don't do it again,' or, 'Think harder next time.' I was beyond all of that. I walked out of the police station shaking.

Worse was yet to come. Mum was onto me the moment I set foot through the door, telling me to pack my bags and get out. I told her to calm down. That really set her off. We got into a slanging match, yelling and swearing at each other. She wasn't going to back down and I didn't have a leg to stand on. I got my stuff together and took off. I figured that she needed a day or two to cool down. I'd call her up and apologise and the whole thing would blow over. It didn't happen like that.

It would be a long time before I was welcome inside Mum's house again.

Some people might think that kicking me out was way too harsh or that it was a risky move. Without parental supervision, I might have ended up going completely off the rails. I don't see it that way. In fact, I have nothing but respect for Mum's decision. It wouldn't have been easy looking your son in the eye and telling him that he is no longer welcome in your home, particularly before he has finished school. The fact that she did it is an indication of how bad things were going for me.

Mum didn't kick me out simply because I was making her life hell or it was convenient. She did it for my benefit. It was the last card in the deck that she could play. She wanted me to grow up, to take responsibility for my actions. Sure, it was a gamble. And although I didn't see it at the time, it was the best thing she could have done.

I'm not saying that I completely cleaned up my act. Subsequent years proved I still had a knack for finding trouble. There will probably always be a bit of that streak in me but I started to think hard about the consequences of my actions. I also started to real-ise that my future was in my own hands. It was high time I made decisions and choices for myself. In other words, it was high time I pulled my bloody head in.

My first decision was to continue on at school. I would've preferred to quit and get a job. The only thing stopping me was a promise I made to Mum years earlier. I vowed to finish school. There were hundreds of times I nearly reneged on the promise. I guess it had become a point of pride – proof that I could finish anything, no matter how much I despised doing it. After getting myself kicked out of home, I had just made the job of finishing school that much harder.

I spent the next seven months crashing on mates' couches and sleeping on floors, living off other people's generosity. I'd do odd jobs for a bit of cash and had more free feeds than I can remember. In the holidays, I managed to snag a proper paying job.

School was still a drag and I didn't exactly knuckle down. I did, however, stop ditching classes all the time. Instead, I only skipped the ones I really hated. My results were terrible. But somehow I scraped through with my leaving certificate.

By the time the results came out I'd already managed to snag a job. It was the worst fucking job I would ever have in my life. My mate Luke Crocker – the one who'd ridden into my house drunk after the winery incident – rang up his grandfather and got me a job gyprocking. He suggested I give it a crack.

Gyprock is a type of plasterboard that is used for walls and ceilings in modern homes. Gyprocking refers to the removal, construction or replacement of this material. I obviously didn't have the qualifications to put the stuff up. So my job was to remove the old stuff. It was horrendous. I'd get sent up into the ceiling on a stinking hot day. Usually I'd be working in a space so cramped I could barely crawl. I'd have to cut away the old gyprock and then feed it down through the ceiling hole. Sometimes the gyprock hadn't been replaced in decades. It would be caked with dust, possum shit, bat shit, spider webs and mould. It was pretty common for entire plasterboards to collapse on top of me, leaving me coated in dust and crap and gasping for air.

I didn't get paid much for that job. But gyprocking taught me a valuable lesson that would come to shape my life: the things you earn through hard work are much more valuable than anything you are given. The money that came from gyprocking wasn't much at all. But they were hard-earned dollars and I didn't spend them easily. I started saving up, rustling up enough cash to get out of South Australia for a fresh start.

My first stop was the Victorian snowfields. Vicki and Dave Dickson, the parents of my mate Phil, made a few phone calls and got me and my other mate Dhani a job at one of the ski lodges at Falls Creek. We worked as house cleaners and did the laundry. I'd be grafting away for hours – tidying up bedrooms, cleaning toilets, changing sheets during the day and doing laundry at night – barely having a moment to see the slopes. But I was enjoying myself. I discovered a work ethic I barely knew existed. I took pleasure in fulfilling a set of daily tasks and getting a financial reward for it.

Making a bit of money was great. But being cooped up indoors all day was wearing thin. I belonged outside. More worrying was the fact the ski season was coming to an end. I needed a job fast.

6

Kings Canyon

I wanted to become a diesel fitter or a boilermaker, someone who manufactured equipment for heavy industry. I'd done well in metal work and woodwork at school. So I asked around. Apprenticeships were hard to come by and it seemed nobody was taking anyone on. There just wasn't enough work.

I got in touch with Lenny Halfpenny, an old family friend who owned a cattle station in Klondyke in northern NSW, and he found me a job on the station. Growing up, Lenny used to have Jono and me up to the station pretty much every summer, and we'd run amok with his kids Darrell and Wayne. Darrell and I became great mates and Lenny was like a second father, teaching me the lay of the land on a cattle station.

I hadn't been to the station for a little while but was planning a visit when I got the devastating news that Darrell had died. Returning home from his pipeline job, his car had rolled on a dirt road about 100 kilometres from the station. Darrell was thrown out the passenger window, crushing his head, and killed instantly. At the time I struggled to understand why such an energetic keen young fella could be killed. He'd had his head screwed on straight and a great career ahead of him. It certainly cemented in my head that life is short.

I loved working at the station and seeing Lenny, but it always saddened me that Darrell wasn't around. Lenny had taken me on as a ringer – a roustabout on a cattle station who does all the jobs nobody else wants to do. I was thrilled. More and more, it felt like a path was opening up before me. It was not, though, as yet completely clear. But one thing I knew for certain: I was not cut out for a desk job. I belonged in the great outdoors. Working on a cattle station seemed like a good fit for me.

I reckon Lenny was pretty surprised to see the transformation that had come over me since I'd left school. There was a fire in my belly, an absolute determination to succeed. I'd push myself harder than anyone, keen to learn as much as possible and build up some experience. When Lenny taught me how to put up fence railing with a chainsaw, shovel and a crowbar, I'd do my utmost to exceed his expectations. When he'd send me out to muster sheep and cattle on the back of a motorbike, I'd drive that bike harder and faster than anyone.

Lenny was a great mentor to me. He taught me farming techniques that I still apply to this day. But it was the practical stuff he passed on that I valued so much, and still do. He also handed down some great life lessons, like the importance of making mistakes. He taught me this lesson the day I ripped up a whole lot of piping with a backhoe while trying to clear off some old fences. Water started bubbling up to the ground. I raced off to the house to turn off the water main before fronting up to Lenny. I was filthy with myself for not having checked that there wasn't any piping under ground. I was half expecting Lenny to fire me.

'Matty,' he said, 'if you aren't making mistakes, you aren't trying.'

For a bloke like me who had developed a fear of failure, it was exactly what I needed to hear. I went back out to help fix the damage to the pipes, wondering why none of my teachers ever taught me that lesson at school.

***

After working on Lenny's station for a summer, I landed a job working in maintenance up in Kings Canyon Resort, in the Northern Territory. There was a downside to my newfound appetite to succeed. I was determined to prove myself stronger, faster, fitter and generally better than everyone else. In the macho culture of the outback, that sort of attitude was always going to land me in a few dust-ups.

Just like at school, I was always puffing out my chest at anyone who gave me shit or looked at me the wrong way. The difference up at Kings Canyon was the size of my opponents. I was coming up against a lot of seriously tough blokes who had seen jacked-up little pricks a hundred times before. I took more than a few hidings.

Fighting wasn't my only problem – I hadn't shaken off the bad-boy behaviour of my schooldays. There was one bloke working at the resort who really pissed me off. Our paths crossed every time I was rostered in the bar in the restaurant, which happened from time to time. I haven't got a very good reason for doing what I did to the bloke – he just struck me as a little snivelling backstabber who was always dobbing staff in to management. When he whispered under his breath that I didn't have a clue how to serve a drink, I decided to teach him a lesson.

To get around the resort, most of us had our own bicycles. This bloke was no different. He owned the latest model, top-of-the-line mountain bike. He absolutely cherished the thing. If I wanted to piss him off the best way was to mess with his bike.

So, in the dead of night, I crept out of my bedroom and went to the maintenance store to get a pair of bolt-cutters and a length of rope. Then I walked to the resort's bike rack. After cutting the bloke's bike free, I wheeled it quietly out to one of the resort's tennis courts. I stopped underneath one of the light towers there and looked up.

The light tower was a 10-metre pole crowned with a large, overhanging lamp that jutted out about a metre at a right angle. This would work just fine. I attached the rope to the bike and tied the other end around my waist. Then I climbed up the tower with the bike hanging beneath me. The tricky part was hauling myself to the very top of the tower and sitting astride the lamp, one leg dangling either side. I carefully balanced myself while untying the rope around my waist. I then looped the rope around the light tower and tied it fast. Satisfied that the knot would hold, I shimmied back down the pole. Once I was safely on the ground, I looked up. The bike was dangling about a metre below the lamp. I smiled all the way back to bed.

I woke up the next morning to a huge commotion. The fella was livid, convinced that someone had stolen his bike. He started hurling accusations everywhere. All non-essential staff members were sent to look for his bike. It was absolutely ridiculous. You would have thought a terrorist had planted a bomb somewhere. Not that I minded. I loved every minute of it.

Eventually, word came through that the bike had been found. I remember heading out to the tennis court with a couple of others and finding old mate staring up at the bike, mouth agape.

'How the hell did it get up there?' he asked.

It took every ounce of restraint not to piss myself laughing. A half-hearted attempt to retrieve the bike was mounted. But it was quickly called off when it was discovered that the resort didn't have a ladder that could extend high enough to reach the bike.

Management was pissed off, too. Nobody stepped forward to claim responsibility, but everyone knew it was me. I had made no great secret of my dislike for the guy and I was the only person physically capable of doing something like that. Sure enough, a day after the discovery of the bike, Jodie – my boss – called me in to her office.

'Matty,' she said, 'I know it was you.'

I kept quiet.

'I don't have any proof that you did it,' she went on. 'But I want you to get that bike down. I don't care how. I just want it down by tomorrow.'

I gave her a half-smile, shrugged and left. That night, I crept back out to the tennis court with a large hunting knife. I looked around to make sure the coast was clear. Then I climbed back to the top of the light tower. I pulled out my knife, and cut the rope. The bike fell like a stone. It didn't just smash when it hit the ground. It detonated. Wheels, spokes, gears and pieces of the alloy frame went everywhere. The bloke was fuming when he found his bike destroyed. But what could he do? There wasn't a shred of evidence that connected me to the bike. It was the perfect crime.

* * *

That wasn't the only bloke I went after. When I discovered one of the resort employees was with my ex-girlfriend, I hosed him down with the hotel's fire extinguisher in the middle of the night. I didn't have a right to complain or to be pissed off – I'd broken it off with her. I just didn't like the idea of someone getting the better of me. I guess I had a few anger issues to work out.

I was pretty fit in those days. I also had a reputation for being a bit of a hothead, so most people kept their distance. But there was one time I picked a fight with the wrong bloke. His name was Shane. He was my best mate out at Kings Canyon and an absolute mad bastard.

Shane was the head chef at the resort. Although he was about 10 years older than me, we hit it off straight away. He wasn't only a talented cook, he was also interested in fitness. This was a guy who knew how to handle himself in the boxing ring. Shane and I used to train together in the resort's gym. He taught me how to box and used to slap me around in the process. One time, he let his other training partner loose on me. I was properly stitched up. His name was Steve and he was a full-blown meathead. If you weren't fighting Steve, you would think he didn't have a bad bone in his body. He was just a big friendly giant with a heart of gold. If you stirred him up, it was a different story. Steve was genuinely scary.

Shane had us together sparring one day. It was supposed to be a friendly workout. We were throwing half-jabs with barely enough power to bring up a bruise. That was until one of my jabs got Steve on the point of the nose. Steve's eyes glazed over and his face went bright red. He charged me like a raging bull, throwing these giant haymakers. I was quick, running him around and telling him to calm down. But Steve had lost control. The only thing that would have made him stop is if he'd collapsed with exhaustion or laid me out. Unfortunately for me, Steve was fitter than

I'd thought. He landed a beautiful uppercut that lifted me right off the ground. The next thing I remember was Shane standing over me, slapping me gently in the face. Steve was standing alongside looking genuinely remorseful.

Steve was big and powerful and had a habit of losing the plot. But he wasn't dangerous like Shane. I discovered that firsthand when I pushed him too far. I guess you could say I had it coming. I was being an absolute pest one night after work, punching him in the arm every time he tried to drink his beer.

'Cut that out,' he said, in a cold tone.

Rather than stop, I upped the ante. I went to my bedroom and brought out my BB gun.

'If you shoot me with that thing,' he said, 'I'll stab you.'

I laughed, thinking he was making a hollow threat and aimed for his leg.

'I'm serious,' he said, completely calm. 'I will fucking stab you.'

I shot him and then backed away in case he came after me. Shane roared like a wounded animal. He pushed back his chair and went off towards the restaurant. I followed him from a distance, laughing my head off, wondering what he was up to. He then reappeared holding a huge knife, his face bright red.

I ran towards my bedroom, stealing a quick glance over my shoulder and catching sight of Shane with his knife raised up high above his head. I made it to my bedroom and locked the door. The knife came through the cheaply made door and stopped inches from my head. I pushed my weight up against the door and braced myself as Shane tried to beat the thing down. He kicked it with all his force. Every so often, he'd drive the knife through the door to where he assumed I was standing. It's a miracle he didn't impale one of my hands. But the real challenge was holding him back when he started taking running jumps at the door. After 45 minutes, the door was hanging by a single hinge.

I started looking about the room for a shield to fend off the attacks if Shane got through the door. At the moment I thought I was about to be killed, Shane stopped. I don't know why. Maybe someone on the other side of the door heard the commotion and called the boss in. Maybe he had injured his shoulder after smashing it into the door for nearly an hour. Whatever the reason, he'd made his point. I never shot him with a BB gun again.

* * *

Work at the Canyon was tough. Management would push you hard during work hours and then leave you to your own devices after. We all partied hard in the hours we had off. There was only one requirement: you had to be right to work the next day. Ninety-nine per cent of the time I was. But there were a couple of instances when I wasn't. One such occasion happened after a full day of maintenance. I had finished off with some drinks at the shed. Then I got called in last minute to fill in a shift at the restaurant that night. And I rolled into work completely drunk.

'I don't think I'm right today,' I said. 'I'm pissed as a fart.'

'Too bad,' said the manager. 'We need you.'

I lasted about an hour before I spilt a tray of drinks over a guest. The manager charged up to me.

'I told you I wasn't right to work,' I said.

The manager was not impressed. Christ knows how I lasted as long as I did at that place. I was lucky to have befriended people like Shane, Jodie and Pete, my boss in the maintenance facility. Those guys had influence. But there was another time when not even my friends could save me.

64

It was the same old problem – boredom and booze. I'd go looking for ways to burn off energy and entertain myself. On the night in question, me and another bloke decided to play a prank on the staff. In the very early hours of the morning, after a night of serious drinking, we burst into every employee's room and set the fire extinguishers on them. They were extinguishers designed to put out electrical fires, spraying a fine white powder rather than water. The mess took days to clean up. I was dragged before management and read the riot act. I didn't get fired. But it was clear they didn't want me around. I didn't care. The time was right for me to move on. Working on a resort was doing my head in by then. There was only one question – what was I to do now?

There's nothing worse than going out in life with nothing to fall back on. I had a solid work ethic and had proven that I could pick things up quickly. It's true that I had a habit of getting into trouble. But buried deep inside was a thirst to succeed. The idea that my life would amount to nothing terrified me.

I thought about becoming a plumber for a while. The resort contracted a plumbing company to come in and do routine maintenance. I had spoken to one of the plumbers and he told me you could make decent money. He even offered to take me on. So I resigned from Kings Canyon and moved to nearby Alice Springs and started work as an apprentice.

It was horrible work. I was paired up with a guy twice my age. This bloke turned out to have a hot temper and a police record a mile long – I found out later that he had done time for armed robbery. He was also worried that I was going to take his job. It was the worst possible outcome. As an apprentice, you expect to be ordered around a bit. But this fella made it his mission to make my life hell.

We would go out on a job somewhere. When we'd arrive, he'd give me a pickaxe and send me off to the wrong place to dig for the pipe. The baked red earth around Alice Springs is harder than concrete. I'd be toiling away in the scorching heat, digging for a pipe that didn't exist. The prick would come out hours later, scream at me that I was digging in the wrong place and then set me up in the right spot. I lasted a couple of weeks before I quit that job.

Plumbing wasn't the right job for me anyway. I needed a job where I could channel my endless amounts of energy, something that involved the outdoors and the use of my hands. Ideally, it would be something I could turn into a career. But most of all, I was looking for an adventure. There were two jobs that came up. Both turned out to be exactly what I was after.

7

A Digger and a Drill Rigger

I applied for the army not long before leaving Kings Canyon. People had been suggesting I join up for years. They probably figured that a young man with bush and shooting skills, bucket loads of energy and who constantly got into fights would be a natural born soldier. Or maybe they thought the army would straighten me out. I only started seriously considering the idea when things started unravelling at the resort.

On the face of it, the army seemed like a good fit for me. I had applied for the air force and the army when I left school, but my grades weren't there for the air force and the army told me to get some life skills and then come back. So there I was, coming back. I wasn't nervous about the physical demands of being in the army or even the possibility of deployment. For someone hell-bent on proving himself the toughest, fittest and strongest bloke going around, landing in a warzone was an exciting prospect.

The army was also a place where I could forge a career. I could see myself climbing the chain of command, maybe even ending up as an officer. Sure, there were risks. Wearing a uniform and kowtowing to superior officers didn't really appeal. But I figured that if things didn't work out I could just apply for something else. Having served in the army looks good on your CV, too. What I didn't know was that getting out of the army was easier said than done.

A couple of corporals interviewed me in Alice Springs. I thought it was all going to be a formality – that they would simply tick a couple of boxes and I would be in. But the army took an age to respond to my application. In the intervening period, I found employment in an unlikely industry. I was going to be a driller.

The idea first popped into my head when I saw those big road-train convoys loaded up with drill rigs and other machinery rolling through Alice Springs. There was something enticing about driving off the map and setting up a rig for weeks on end. I started asking around, bailing up drillers in pubs and asking about life on a rig. I immediately liked what I was hearing.

The job offered good wages and there was also the potential for career advancement. The blokes I spoke to warned me that I would be working to tight schedules in the extreme heat. There was also extensive training involved. I'd have to learn how to drive heavy freight and operate a front-end loader, not to mention getting my driller's ticket.

But they didn't tell me everything. I had to work out for myself that some drillers are different characters. It's pretty obvious when you think about it. A job that involves working in remote, inhospitable places for weeks on end is going to draw some colourful characters. Not that I was worried. It was becoming more obvious to me that I wasn't suited to a normal life. The idea of holding down a nine-to-five job in the city held no appeal. I needed adventure.

So I applied for work with a whole lot of drilling companies. I snagged a government job with the Northern Territory's Department of Land Resource Management. Sure enough, I got the drilling job the same day the army told me that I'd been accepted as a recruit. I rang up the army, told them my predicament. They suggested I enlist in the Army Reserves.

'You still have to complete a three-month training course,' I was told. 'From there you'll be required to serve a certain number of days each year.'

They told me it was good that I'd landed a government job. Private companies are less scrupulous when it comes to approving leave for reservists. There is usually better oversight in the public service. But I decided to hold off my training in the army. I figured that my new employer wouldn't be pleased if I took off on day one for three months of training. I told the army of my decision and went drilling.

* * *

Bore water is one Australia's great natural resources. At 1.7 million square kilometres in size, Australia's Great Artesian Basin is the largest confined aquifer in the world, holding an estimated 65 000 cubic kilometres of ground water. It sits below some of the most remote country on the planet. That meant driving a bloody long way into unexplored places. The job description was to discover and define groundwater resources across the Territory through water bore drilling. If deemed viable, the ground water would be used for irrigation.

We were headquartered in Darwin, the only state capital in the world allowing 'quads' – a road train comprising a prime mover towing four trailers – to within a kilometre of the central business district. I'd generally be operating a quad or a triple, which had the same configuration as a quad minus a trailer. Our operating window was throughout the dry season, before the rains turned the roads into lakes. We'd work in four-man teams, working full throttle for months on end. We drilled the length and breadth of the Northern Territory. One job might be right down near the South Australian border, the next could be a 1700-kilometre, two-day drive to the eastern edge of Arnhem Land.

Some people hated the driving, whereas that was the part I loved the most. There was something liberating about rolling across dirt roads, casting an eye on country that very few people get to see, country music blasting in the cab. As a 19-year-old, it was a powerful feeling. But there were a few nervous moments on those drives. One particular incident stands out above the rest.

It happened on the return trip from a 13-week job on the northwestern tip of the Territory, near Murganella. The job itself had been good. I had volunteered as camp custodian. The camp custodian remains on site to maintain the camp and grease the machine while the other boys return home. Being alone in the outback without human contact for weeks on end can send some people mad. Not me, though. I'd just gone through a nasty break-up. Time on my own was just what I needed.

The maintenance of the machines only took me about an hour each day. Then I'd be off fishing, chasing crocs down in the shallows, shooting wild pigs, cooking up my food on a campfire. It was the ultimate freedom. My only contact with civilisation was the daily call I was supposed to make on an old high-frequency radio that turned out to be faulty. I was radioing in, but they couldn't hear me. I only found that out when a ranger from Kakadu turned up to tell me that police had me listed as missing.

But there was no real harm done. The ranger called off the search and remained in the camp for a day. When the drillers returned to pack up, I was feeling fit and reinvigorated. Unexpectedly, things came unstuck on the trip home.

It was very late in the year and the wet season was around the corner. We packed up the rig, loaded our road trains and then headed back to Darwin. I was towing two large trailers, a medium trailer and a smaller two-wheel trailer known as a dog trailer. About an hour into the trip, the storm hit. There was so much water on the road, my wheels started to lose traction. It felt like I was driving on ice. Our lead driver got on the radio.

'Nobody stops!' he shouted. 'If we stop in this shit, we'll get bogged.'

So on we ploughed. I was fighting the wheel, working hard to keep the truck on the road. I dropped down a gear, hopeful that at a slower speed I'd hold the road better. But the road was turning into a river. There were sections where the water came up to the top of my tyres. If I dropped my speed too dramatically, I'd get bogged. So I floored the accelerator. In retrospect, something was bound to go wrong.

The first warning I had was losing one of my trailers. The sound of it coming loose was like thunder booming above the roar of the truck's engine. I looked out the window and saw my dog trailer – which was carrying all the fuel – aquaplaning off the road. I slowed down but the dog trailer's inertia carried it forward and was dragging my second trailer off the road too. From above, it would have looked like a giant metallic arm extending through the bush, clearing away scrub and trees. It was only a matter of time before one of those trailers tipped over. If that happened, the entire road train would be turned over. With all the fuel I was carrying, I'd be cooked.

I put the foot down on the accelerator in the hope of dragging her back into line. It had no effect. The dog trailer was acting with a mind of its own. It started to inch forward so that it was level with the front of the cab. It felt like I was in a drag race. I didn't dare adjust my speed. If I slowed too much, the dog trailer would speed past me and pull me off the road. If I tried outpacing the dog trailer and accelerated, I risked losing control completely. Luckily there were no tall gums lining the side of the road. If the trailer snagged a tree, the road train would be ripped apart. When a road train crashes at speed, the driver rarely survives. All I could do was hang on and hope.

The rain eased a little, slightly improving visibility. The road ahead appeared to be clearing of water. But there was a worrying development. The side of the road was dropping away. I was now noticeably higher than the dog trailer. Maybe it was my imagination, but it felt as if the cab was starting to lean to one side.

I looked ahead and swore. About 200 metres ahead, the side of the road dropped down into a large ditch. In about three seconds the dog trailer would fall into the ditch and the show would be over. For a split second, I contemplated opening my driver's door and leaping out. The road train was travelling at over 60 km/h and the side of the road was hard and rocky.

About 50 metres before disaster, the dog trailer hit a dry section. I felt the front cab shudder as the trailer's tyres gripped the road and swung back in line. I dropped my speed. I was worried that the trailer's little excursion on the side of the road would have damaged the axle or punctured tyres. There was still a chance it could tip over at any moment. After about 10 minutes, I was confident that the danger had passed.

I fell behind as the convoy sped on to Darwin. I jumped out once I got on some dry ground to inspect the truck and its trailers. Incredibly, the only noticeable damage was a few gashes along the side of the trailer's tyres. Otherwise everything appeared to be fine. I arrived about 30 minutes after the others and decided to keep that one quiet and not tell the boss what had happened.

* * *

The job involved more than just drilling for bore water. Sometimes the department sent us out to do repair work. The most interesting jobs involved fixing damage done by prospectors who'd headed into the red centre looking for oil or natural gas. This was in the early days of exploration drilling. Back then, mechanised vehicles weren't built to go off road. So they loaded primitive drilling equipment onto the backs of camels, picked a point on the compass and went in search for their fortune.

It was costly, time-consuming and dangerous work. These blokes were often heading into barren country that had never been explored. There didn't seem to be much logic to where they dug their holes. There seemed to be only one guiding principle – the more remote the better.

My most memorable repair job happened in the heart of the Simpson Desert. Eighty years earlier, exploration drillers had punched a hole in the earth's surface hoping to find oil. Instead, they found the Artesian Basin. They abandoned the site after water bubbled up instead of black gold and were either unable or unwilling to plug the hole. The department was worried that the water was still gushing out. Our brief was to cap the hole.

From Alice Springs, we drove south for 10 hours to the town of Finke and stopped overnight. At first light, we headed due east across the rolling sand dunes, following a GPS location. It was slow going. Road trains have a long braking distance because of the huge tonnage they haul. That meant we had to keep the trucks in a low gear just in case we had to stop suddenly. There was, after all, no way of telling if we were approaching a boulder or a sudden dip in the road.

On and on we went, heading for a little pinprick in the desert. We came to our destination in the early afternoon. It was somewhere near the intersection of the Queensland/South Australia/ Northern Territory border. This was the absolute definition of the middle of nowhere.

I'll never forget cresting that last sand dune and casting my eyes on one of the most spectacular and beautiful sights I've seen in my life. The hole those prospectors dug had created an oasis. Around the hole, there were a few hundred metres of native grass and shrubs. As we approached, birds took flight from trees that grew around a large network of lagoons and pools that had formed from the run-off. It was like a Garden of Eden in the Simpson Desert.

In the middle of the oasis, we found the fountain of water bubbling away. It was a shame we had to put a cap on that hole. The moment the ground water stopped gushing to the surface, this pristine ecosystem would start dying. But this wasn't a natural phenomenon. It was man-made. That hole needed to be plugged. The question was how to do it.

The first task was to check the head pressure and measure the volume of water that was gushing up. To do that, we had to build a large platform above the hole, allowing us to lower a remote camera down to get a closer look. It was dangerous work. The water was coming up from deep below the earth's surface. It was piping hot. If anyone fell in they would be scalded.

On closer inspection, we saw that the people who had drilled this hole had attempted to cap it. But the steel casing had rusted out over the years and was woefully inadequate. We calculated that 50 litres a second was bubbling out of that hole. A disintegrated steel cap was never going to hold out against that sort of pressure. This was a job that needed a modern solution.

First of all, we widened the breach with the drill pipe to reduce the pressure. We concreted the area around the hole before lowering an enormous nine-by-nine-metre casing. The casing was in two parts – an outer square and then a much smaller inner section – that had been welded together. One of the boys was working the crane, levering the casing down with the aid of guide ropes while the boss shouted instructions from the edge of the platform. The rest of us huddled off to the side, waiting with bated breath.

The crane lowered the cap into place and the water flow abruptly stopped. We had just enough time to congratulate each other on a job well done before everything went to shit.

The pressure blew the inner casing away and a huge column of steaming hot water shot into the air. Fifty litres a second was now being pumped through a hole with an eight-inch diameter and splashing onto the platform. My boss was knocked off his feet and washed beneath the platform. He tried to get out of the hole, but the water was pouring down on him. He was going to drown. The bloke on the crane, meanwhile, had abandoned ship. He was worried that the entire rig was going to collapse.

I jumped up on the platform and gritted my teeth as hot water splashed against my skin. I slipped over on the sodden wooden platform and ran over to the crane controls. I pulled back on the levers, lifting the casing off the hole, thereby reducing the pressure. The waterspout vanished and the hole went back to a bubbling hot spring. While I lifted off the cap the other boys helped the boss up. He looked like he'd been sunbaking on a beach without sunscreen. He was lucky he wasn't killed.

8

Kapooka

After six months drilling, I felt I'd established myself in the job. It was time for me to join the army. I made a few phone calls and managed to get into a training module that coincided with the wet season. The boss was happy. Losing me through the off-season was no big deal. In electing to do my training through the hottest time of the year, I was asking for a tough slog. But I figured that after a year of drilling, I could handle tough situations.

Everyone who takes the 10-kilometre bus trip from Wagga Wagga in New South Wales to Kapooka has a similar story. The NCOs – sergeants and corporals – meet you outside the bus and are all smiles and handshakes. They act like your best mates, reassuring you that you've made the best decision of your life. Then you pull into Blamey Barracks – the army's recruit training centre – and everything goes to shit.

This is exactly what I experienced. The bus came to a stop and a sergeant stood up, a dark shadow falling across his face. He eyeballed everyone on the bus before drawing in a lungful of air.

'RECRUITS!' he roared. 'GET OFF THIS BUS! NOW!'

After all the backslapping we'd just gone through, I initially thought he was taking the piss. I started laughing out loud. Big mistake.

'WHAT ARE YOU LAUGHING AT, MAGGOT? GET OFF THIS BUS, NOW!'

We all scurried off the bus and sort of huddled together like a bunch of scared children. The sergeant absolutely blasted us, telling us to properly form two lines. Eventually, when that was sorted out, we had to hand over our phones and any contraband – knives, cigarettes, food, and whatever else. All our personal items were shoved into bags. Then we were directed to our barracks. Each recruit was issued a camouflage uniform and physical training (PT) gear. We were ordered to change into our PT gear and prepare for our first march. It was stinking hot weather – high 30s, without a breath of wind. We marched back and forth across the parade ground for hours on end. The NCOs were relentless.

'We don't stop until everyone marches in step,' they said.

The moment I missed a step or tripped, a sergeant or a corporal would be in his or her face, hurling abuse. It took us three hours before we all found our rhythm. Before being dismissed, we were warned that there would be plenty of marching in the coming weeks.

That night in the mess hall, everyone was assigned to a room, four people to each. A six-foot-high divider ran down the middle of the room for greater privacy and each person was assigned a locker that had to be kept in pristine condition. Lights-out was at 10 o'clock.

Most recruits will tell you that the first night is daunting. Reality dawns when those lights are switched off. This was where we would be stuck for the next 80 days. Most recruits are fresh-faced kids just out of school. I didn't hear anyone break down and cry on that first night, but I'm sure it happened. After an afternoon of marching, I was too exhausted to care. I fell into a deep sleep.

In the morning I was wrenched awake by the sound of machine-gun fire.

'What the fuck was that?' asked one of my roommates.

Off it went again. I stayed completely still while another round was fired. The first morning reveille was being announced with machine-gun fire in the hallway. They were firing blanks, of course. But it's not the best 6 a.m. start. This was the morning alarm bell, Australian army-style.

'GET OUT OF BED!' roared the sergeant down the corridor. 'GET UP! GET UP!'

We'd been briefed the night before on what was to supposed to happen each morning. We had to tear the sheets off our bed and then form up in the corridor. Once everyone was accounted for, it was on.

'GET MOVING!'

We had 15 minutes to make our bed to army standard, fight for a shower, shave, get dressed and then wait for inspection. The sergeant barked, roared, screamed, shouted and humiliated practically all of us that morning. Everyone had to remake his bed. As punishment we went without breakfast, and were sent back out onto the parade ground to go marching.

I was suddenly struck with the feeling that I'd made a terrible mistake in coming here. I couldn't believe I turned my back on a job that I enjoyed to come to this place and get treated like a schoolkid. I would have walked off the barracks right then if not for one compelling reason to stay – I would have been arrested. The NCOs made a point of reminding us that the moment we'd signed up, we'd effectively handed ourselves over to the military.

'By all means, leave,' they used to taunt. 'You'll be thrown into jail.'

Not only was the jail term longer than the three-month training course, you'd also have a record. It made sense that going AWOL was deemed a serious offense. But I couldn't believe how heavily recruits were punished for offences that in normal life you'd consider pretty minor stuff.

Take pulling a sickie, for example. This was something the army classified as 'malingering', aka a chargeable offence. I heard that the only way you could get out of the training was if you told the padre you were going to kill everyone on the base. They'd put you on the first bus out of there. But you also ran the risk of being charged by the police.

So I was trapped in this place for three months. The letters I was writing back to Mum started out being very negative. 'My sergeant is a cockhead!' I'd write. 'I want to get out of this bloody place.' But then something strange happened. I started to enjoy myself.

* * *

At Kapooka, we were told that the infantry – soldiers who fight on foot – are an elite group. Only the best are admitted. To become the best, you have to train the hardest. I'd done jobs that had challenging moments – working as a ringer on a cattle station, working in maintenance on a resort, cleaning toilets and bedrooms in ski lodges and drilling bores across the country. I'd had my share of long, tough days. But this was different.

Every morning began with physical training – pack marches mainly, over long distances. In the first couple of weeks, we'd walk three kilometres, lugging rifles, 10-kilogram packs and full webbing – the military belts, packs and pouches soldiers wear to store rations, water, ammunition, first aid, survival equipment and much more.

The mornings became more gruelling the deeper into the training we progressed. Before the end of the first month, we were lugging 15-kilo packs, seven kilos of webbing and machine guns over 20 kilometres. We were walking across uneven ground in temperatures that soared into the high 30s. Inevitably, people started to come unstuck.

Those first few weeks were undoubtedly the toughest for all of us. The people who struggled the most were those who were stuck in a civilian mindset. This wasn't like normal life, nor was it a normal job. The trick was to adjust to the surroundings and form a different definition of what constituted a tough day. Only then can you really appreciate how far the human body can be pushed.

I was learning lessons of my own. Top of the list was the importance of teamwork. We'd all been grouped into platoons – a unit-size of about 27 – and then split into sections of nine. As a section, you would do almost everything together, from weapons training to eating meals. It bred intense camaraderie. Those eight other people would become like family. If one person in your section fell back on the march, then the rest of you would stay back with him or her. It became clear to us all that you are only as strong as your weakest link. This lesson stood me in good stead when I started my own businesses.

Outward appearance counts for nothing. Big, burly blokes

who talked tough were more likely to whinge and cry than anyone else. Often, it was the skinny, little fellas that would excel – never complaining, but instead encouraging the ones that showed signs of cracking. Most surprising to me were the female recruits. They were treated as harshly as the rest of us and I don't remember seeing one of them lose it. At Kapooka, mental toughness counted for more than physical ability.

Life at Kapooka wasn't all torture. In fact, there were elements I really enjoyed. Weapons training was great fun. It's not every day you get to fire a machine gun or a grenade launcher. The weapons-training simulation system – a 12-lane indoor small-arms facility where you learnt to shoot with laser guns in a computer-generated virtual reality – was a particular highlight.

Everything we did – the physical conditioning, pack marching, weapons training, bayonet drills, building camaraderie – was all a prelude to what I felt was the main event: the war games. The games took place towards the end of our training. We went bush for three days loaded up with rations and survival equipment. Our mission was to ambush and capture opposing platoons.

This seemed to me to be the right sort of training. It was the complete opposite to how I felt about parade drill. Essentially, our training was in preparation for combat. What good was being able to march in step or salute a superior officer when bullets are whizzing around your head? The answer I got back whenever I asked this question always referred to discipline, the one area in life I'd always struggled with.

The army principle of saluting someone's rank rather than the individual was something that rang hollow. I just couldn't respect someone if they were on a power trip, no matter their rank. It was an attitude that got me in strife. On one memorable occasion,

I was severely punished for talking back to a sergeant during a stifling hot parade drill. He was giving everyone a hard time and really getting off on it. Eventually, I came in for some attention.

'Recruit!' he roared, a couple of inches from my nose. 'Your uniform is dirty! Why is it dirty?'

I kept silent.

'Wright!' he persisted. 'Why is your uniform dirty?'

'Get stuffed,' I said.

The sergeant's face turned red and spittle started forming at the corners of his mouth. He was so stunned that he was literally lost for words. I thought he was going to take a swing, which I would've welcomed. *Just give me one excuse to punch you*, I thought.

Eventually he found his voice. I was blasted for about five minutes and then told to report to the CO's office. I waited outside while the sergeant got together with the other NCOs to work out what to do with me. About an hour later I was called back onto the parade ground. To make an example of my insubordination, my punishment was shouted out so that everyone could hear. I was made to camp in my swag outside the CO's office for a week. While everyone ate, I was expected to march on my own back and forth across the parade ground. For food, I would eat pack rations, which had a reputation for being disgusting. The week was made that much worse because it coincided with a period of sustained rain.

I was always getting into trouble. Sometimes the reasons were just flat out ridiculous. One time, I ended up getting lumped with extra duty for misplacing my jocks. Nobody would have known were it not for the fact that I lost them on the day we were being taught how to dress in uniform. It was a pretty involved exercise.

A corporal assembled each platoon in a room and then told us all to drop our pants. I hesitated.

'Wright!' shouted the corporal. 'What are you doing? Drop your trousers.'

Both male and female recruits looked in my direction. I shrugged my shoulders and dropped my dacks. Everyone, except the corporal, started laughing when they saw I was free balling. I thought it was all a bit of harmless fun, until I came in for more disciplining.

Being back in a highly regimented institution seemed to draw out the rebel in me. Just like during my school days, I was a magnet for individuals who got a thrill from doing exactly what we were told not to do. One such person was one of my dorm mates, who I will call Wilson.

One Friday night, after a particularly arduous week of training, Wilson and I decided we needed a beer. We got into full dress uniform, snuck out of the barracks and found the NCO's wet mess. This was the bar for Kapooka's corporals and sergeants. It was strictly off limits to recruits. So Wilson and I had to play our part – we were Sergeant Wright and Corporal Wilson for the night. Nobody seemed to notice we didn't have the appropriate number of chevrons on our shoulders to gain entry. It was probably because everyone was so pissed. Luckily, none of our instructors came down for a drink.

We spent the night chatting up the army girls and getting completely smashed. We staggered back to the barracks and slipped into our dorm room in the wee hours. We got away with it that time. But there were times we pushed our luck too far.

* * *

While frantically cleaning everything up in our room before an inspection, Wilson made a mockery of the army tradition of keeping clean socks turned up. We were supposed to fold our socks in such a way so that they formed a smile. Don't ask me why. Wilson obviously thought the whole tradition was stupid. He started pretending that his upturned socks were giving him a blowjob. He even pulled his dick out of his trousers. The rest of us in the room thought it was hilarious. The sound of our laughter drew the attention of the sergeant, who burst into our room with a corporal standing either side.

'Recruit!' shouted the sergeant. 'What do you think you are doing?'

Wilson stood to attention, doing his best to keep the smile off his face, as the sergeant pulled away his socks leaving his dick hanging out of his trousers. I got up on the cupboard behind the NCOs and threw down another pair of socks.

'Cover yourself up, recruit!' I bellowed.

Wilson, me and our two dorm mates were all placed on reduced rations and instructed to do extra marching for a couple of weeks. How I got through the whole thing without being discharged is a mystery.

* * *

Mum came up for the march out parade – the Kapooka term for the passing out parade. She was absolutely bursting with pride. She took one look at me in my dress uniform, clean shaven and fitter than I'd ever been in my life, and started to cry. I felt a genuine sense of satisfaction from completing the course. At that point, it was the greatest achievement of my life.

One of the NCOs approached Mum and predicted I'd go full

time in the army. It was intended as a compliment and I appreciated him saying it to Mum. But I knew in my heart that I'd never go full time. I'll admit, there were times at Kapooka when I had given it serious thought. I was inspired when a couple of SAS guys came into our barracks and spoke to us about service in Australia's elite special operations force. It was hard not to be in awe of those guys. Stories of SAS training were legendary – a whole different level of hardship and endurance compared to Kapooka.

One SAS guy actually approached me. It turned out that a couple of the instructors had identified me as a person that might fit the mould of an SAS soldier. It was a genuine honour to be singled out in that way, and the SAS soldier made an impressive pitch. He'd obviously done background research on me, because he started off talking about how boring and pointless he found marching on the parade ground. He said that not much of that sort of stuff was done in the SAS. He then went on to congratulate me on my scores in the shooting drills and asked if I was interested in becoming a sniper.

He told me that going up to Regiment, as they call it, was no cakewalk. In fact, statistically, I was unlikely to make it. Training was based on weeding out the ones that didn't have what it took to be the best of the best.

'You probably won't get in,' he said. This guy was hitting all the right buttons. At that time in my life, if you said I couldn't do something, I'd go out of my way to prove you wrong. But something held me back from going down the SAS path. I guess I just didn't like the idea of being flung from warzone to warzone and sent out on operations to kill people.

So I returned to my drilling job in Darwin. The Army Reserve assigned me to North-West Mobile Force (NORFORCE), the Top

End's reserve infantry regiment. Just like at Kapooka, there were elements I really enjoyed. Doing exercises throughout Arnhem Land, firing rocket launchers and testing claymores – highly explosive anti-personnel mines – was great fun. But the same things that bugged me at Kapooka were just as infuriating with NORFORCE.

It felt like every other Thursday I was heading out to Darwin's Larrakeyah Barracks, marching back and forth in the blazing heat and shouting out, 'Yes, sir!' every five seconds. My sergeant made matters worse. He was a complete dickhead on a power trip. When I found out he worked at McDonald's, I knew my time was up. I don't mean to be disrespectful to people who work at a fast food joint, but I found it hard to take orders from some weekend warrior who flipped burgers for a living. Besides, I was beginning to develop a new passion – one that would completely change the course of my life. I wanted to become a chopper pilot.

ABOVE: Some of Mum's mates put me in a horse's bridle near our place in Second Valley, South Australia. Even as a toddler I had to be restrained!

Mum gave me this five-foot carpet snake for my ninth birthday. I named him Solomon and he grew to 11 feet before dying just after I turned 20.

TOP: Sitting at the the bow of a yacht off the coast of Cairns with my hero, Jerry. Jerry's passion for the outdoors was infectious.

My early years were full
of adventure: horse riding,
fishing, swimming and driving
mini four-wheel drives were
all in a day's play.

Mum posing with the monster boar she took down on Kangaroo Island.
Her quarry dwarfed the wild pig I took down years later.

Training to become an infantryman at the Army Recruit Training Centre at Kapooka, one of the toughest experiences of my life.

Enjoying a bath while working on a drill rig in the Northern Territory.

Learning to fly a chopper was hands down the hardest thing I've ever done.

MIDDLE: Dave and Phil Dickson standing alongside Dave's experimental chopper, shortly before the accident. Dave and Phil's death rocked the McLaren Vale community.

BOTTOM: Mum and me with my Robinson R22.

Without question, Mum has been the most influential figure in my life.
There is nobody I admire more.

TOP: Side by side with my sister Holly. It's fair to say we got on each other's nerves growing up, but we've always been great mates.

BOTTOM LEFT: My best mate in the whole world, Naish.

BOTTOM RIGHT: My absolute pride and joy, Brooke. Her passion for wildlife and the outdoors is even greater than mine.

This is early morning after a night of catching crocs
with a harpoon pole. *(National Geographic Australia)*

9

Choppers

I was cleaning the trucks in the drilling yard at Winnellie, a northern suburb of Darwin. It was towards the end of the drilling season, just before the rains arrived. The pressure hose was throwing red dirt and shit all over me and, with all the trucks and trailers in the yard that needed washing, it was going to be a long day. I gritted my teeth, wishing I was anywhere else, when suddenly I became engulfed in dirt and dust.

I looked up. Swooping low overhead was a group of Australian army Kiowa helicopters. The pilots were really throwing them around. I was captivated. I'd always wanted to fly choppers. But two things always held me back: one, I didn't think I was smart enough; and two, I didn't think I'd ever have the money to do it.

Dave Dickson, the father of my schoolmate Phil, had first put the thought of learning to fly choppers in my head years earlier. Dave ran his own tooling business and was an avid helicopter pilot. When I'd last been home, he was designing an experimental helicopter and was already sourcing the parts. Dave's enthusiasm for choppers was infectious, but nothing got my blood flowing quite like seeing mustering pilots in action.

Mustering pilots are vital to the effective management of a cattle station. A chopper is very versatile, capable of reaching places that are inaccessible to land-based vehicles. Back in the day, a team of 12 stockmen and two horse trailers and up to 75 horses would be hobbled out to round up cattle. The stockmen would be gone for over to two weeks, driving cattle over incredible distances. With helicopters, the same job can be done in a single day. Chopper pilots are the drovers of the modern age. The northern part of the country is totally dependent on them to keep the cattle industry afloat. In 2015 alone, nearly 1.3 million head of cattle were exported from Australia. Shifting those sorts of numbers is only made possible because of choppers.

But it's a dangerous job. Over the last decade, around about 15 mustering pilots have died on the job. When you see these pilots in action, it isn't hard to work out why. To do the job of mustering animals from the air, a pilot must fly the helicopter to the absolute limit. They have to operate at very low altitude, which obviously increases the likelihood of crashing. Misread a gust of wind, fail to see a tree or lose your bearings for a split second, and it's all over.

I loved to watch them in action. On my days off from drilling, I would take on extra work as ringer on cattle stations. It was a great way to make a little extra cash and I loved the work. My favourite job was mustering cattle. The station owner would stick me on the back of a quad bike and send me out to assist the mustering pilots drive the cattle or water buffalo into the yard. Seeing those pilots shooting around in their little Robinson R22s was mesmerising. To me, these guys were gods.

The problem was money. Getting a chopper licence would take time and it was hard to make a living as a junior pilot. Financial security had suddenly become important. I was seeing a girl and things were getting serious. She wanted to buy a house and start a family. The idea of settling down drew out anxieties about my ability to provide. I was determined not to have a family that lived paycheck to paycheck. Drilling provided me with a steady income. That seemed more important than anything. That was until the drilling job went to shit.

The turning point was on a job near Daly Waters, 600 kilometres south of Darwin. The incident happened the night after a drinking session in the Daly Waters pub. I had come across a mustering pilot by the name of Phil Irlem who was propped up at the bar. I bought Phil rum for the whole night and peppered him with questions. Phil knew exactly what was going on.

'Mate, you've got to bite the bullet and just do it,' he said.

'What are you talking about?' I said.

'If becoming a mustering pilot is what you want to do, there's no point waiting around.'

I told Phil that my girlfriend and I were already looking around for houses. Becoming a student for a year while I learnt to fly a chopper and then earning a pittance was no way to pay a mortgage.

'I don't mean to be disrespectful,' he said, 'but you're only young. I'm guessing this girlfriend won't be your last.'

I laughed in a sort of dismissive way. But Phil had struck a chord. I wasn't sure I was ready to settle down. The drilling job was stagnating too. I wanted to be progressing faster up the ladder. After more than 18 months in the job, I was still a driller's assistant – that was code for shit kicker. All I was qualified to do was operate a front-end loader and drive a road train. Until I could operate the actual drill rig, my career was stuck in a rut.

I took it up with the head driller the next day. He said I wasn't ready. I reckon he was worried about me taking his job, and I said as much to his face. Things got heated and I ended up taking a swing at him with a 36-inch pipe wrench. It sounds serious, but these sorts of blow-ups happened a lot while drilling. It was a way of sorting out differences and letting off steam. Blokes would often have it out and then everything would return to normal. But this for me was the tipping point.

'I'm not going to fight for this job,' I said. 'You can have it.'

I got a lift back to Daly Waters and hitched a ride to Darwin. I had just kicked a life of financial security to the curb. The funny thing was, I'd never felt better. It was one of those moments of absolute clarity. My future wasn't drilling or working the land. It was flying.

My girlfriend didn't see things quite as clearly. Not only was I unemployed, I was planning to take myself out of the workforce for a year to become a student. There was no way we were buying a house any time soon. It was time to go our separate ways. It was a tough decision but definitely for the best.

I packed my bags, loaded up the car and drove two days straight to the Sunshine Coast. I was heading for Blue Tongue Helicopters – the best chopper school in the country. When I arrived, I walked straight up to the reception desk and enrolled in the full-time program. The course would end up costing me about $40 000. That was every cent in my savings account plus a loan from the bank and my grandmother. It wasn't easy shelling out that sort of cash or taking on debt. But it definitely gave me an incentive to make it work.

I managed to find a cheap place to rent near the chopper school. The night before my first day at the controls of a helicopter, I couldn't take the smile off my face. It wasn't long before that smile turned into a frown. Learning how to fly a helicopter was hands down the hardest thing I've ever had to do.

The people who are drawn to flying helicopters are all cut from the same cloth. I can usually pick the sorts of people who want to learn how to fly helicopters. They are more often than not big-talking blokes interested in cars, bikes and anything mechanical. They are generally accustomed to picking things up quickly and expect the same to happen when it comes to flying.

'I can ride a motorbike, surf, ride horses and operate machinery,' they'll say. 'I'll be able to fly a chopper.'

When I returned to Blue Tongue Helicopters as an instructor years later, I would see the same sort of bloke swagger into the school, talking about how easy it was going to be. I didn't judge them because I was exactly the same. I thought it was going to be a breeze, too.

I was part of an intake of nine other aspiring pilots. Our pre-flight instructor, who taught theory classes in the weeks leading up to our first individual flight, did his best to knock us down to size.

'Flying helicopters is a highly challenging and extremely dangerous occupation,' he said, straight off the bat. 'The stats suggest that one in four helicopter pilots will die on the job.'

The room fell silent. It was a hell of a way to begin our training.

'These days,' he continued, 'the vast majority of accidents are the result of pilot error.'

I wasn't convinced that the stats were accurate. I just figured he was trying to scare us into paying attention. And it worked. All of us buried our heads in the theory, reading the operational handbooks and textbooks cover to cover. Each night, before going to bed, I would imagine myself at the controls, holding the chopper in a hover above the pad, impressing the hell out my instructor. I felt like I had everything sorted. I was ready for the real thing. I was in for a big wake-up call.

I can't remember ever being as excited as I was on the morning I was to fly a helicopter for the first time. I strode out to the chopper waiting for me on the pad. I was going to be trained in an old Bell 47, a vintage helicopter with a distinctive full-bubble canopy and exposed welded-tube tail boom. My trainer was Graeme Gillies. It's no exaggeration to say that Graeme is among the very best helicopter instructors in Australia. He has been flying choppers since the late 1970s and has racked up nearly 17 000 hours' flying time. He cut his teeth as a mustering pilot at Magoura and Victoria River Downs stations.

Graeme was from the old school. I'd already seen him tear strips off more than a handful of students who weren't progressing at the expected rate. I even saw him chase a struggling student across a helicopter pad before throwing his headset at the poor bloke. The student had been at it for months and was showing no signs of improvement. When the student brought the helicopter's tail to within inches of hitting the ground, Graeme lost it. Obviously I was eager to impress. The last thing I wanted was a headset hurled in my direction.

Graeme powered up the chopper and got us airborne. I'd been in choppers on cattle stations before – the thrill of your first ever flight is something you'll never forget. Every part of your body hums as the rotors chop the air above and the engine growls behind you. But this time was different. To think I was actually going take control of this machine was a whole new level of excitement.

The first thing I was going to be taught in training is the hardest thing to master as a chopper pilot – the hover. While hovering, a helicopter generates gusty wind, which acts against the fuselage. To remain steady requires constant, tiny adjustments to the controls. This is far easier said than done.

There are four key control inputs – the cyclic, the collective, the anti-torque pedals and the throttle. The name of each instrument refers to the effect each control has on either the main rotor or the tail rotor. Graeme started me on the pedals.

The pedals control the tail rotor, the function of which is to compensate against the incredible spinning force of the main rotor. Without the tail rotor, the fuselage would spin around uncontrollably beneath the main rotor. This effect is known as torque. To compensate, the tail rotor – also known as the anti-torque rotor – pushes the tail boom against the force of the main blades. Two separate foot pedals control the intensity of the tail rotor's spin. Pushing down on the left pedal will increase intensity, pushing with greater force against the main rotor and turning the nose of the chopper right. The right pedal decreases the resistance allowing the tail boom to turn left with the main rotor.

'Okay, I want you to line up that post directly ahead,' said Graeme. 'Keep us pointed towards the post.'

'Righto,' I said.

'The pedals are yours,' Graeme said.

The moment Graeme handed me control, the post that he had told me to line up disappeared from view as we spun left. I hit the left pedal and the tail boom lurched round to the right. I'd massively overcompensated. The pedals were spongy and took a few critical moments to take effect when pressed. It was like I was constantly playing catch-up, the machine moving a beat before me. It took me a while, but I eventually had the post lined up reasonably steady.

'Not bad,' said Graeme. 'I'm going to take control of the pedals.'

And with that, the chopper instantly steadied.

'Now it's time for the collective,' he said.

The collective is located on the left-hand side of the pilot and is shaped a little like an enlarged handbrake in a car. The effect of pulling up the collective stick is to increase the intensity or pitch of the main rotor blades *collectively*, which in turn increases altitude. Lowering the collective stick drops the pitch and the machine descends. It's simple enough in theory. In practice, it's a different story.

'All right, I want you to take hold of the collective while I handle the other controls. Try and keep us twenty feet off the ground.'

The moment Graeme handed me over the control of the collective, the machine jumped 10 feet. I pushed down hard on the stick, bringing us to within a couple of feet from the ground. Graeme was anticipating this response because he grabbed hold of the collective a split second from disaster and brought us back to a controlled hover.

'Let's try that again,' he said.

We bounced up and down like this for the next few minutes. Imagine learning how to drive manual and bunny hopping down the street. Well, this was 100 times harder. As with the pedals, the secret was to make the smallest possible adjustments. After about five minutes, I held her 20 feet above the ground.

'Okay,' said Graeme. 'I'll take control.'

Graeme reminded me not to forget the twist grip at the end of the collective. The twist grip controls throttle and needs to be coordinated with the up-and-down motion of the collective stick.

'Pulling up the collective increases pitch, which, in turn, requires more throttle or else you might stall,' he said.

Lastly, we came to the cyclic. The cyclic is similar to a joystick. It is called the cyclic because it changes the pitch of the main rotor blades *cyclically*. So, if I were to move the cyclic stick left or right, the main rotor blades would increase their pitch on one side of the cycle and feather on the other side. The result is to lower the spinning disk towards the feathering side of the cycle and therefore provide thrust in that direction. The same applies to the vertical plane – push the cyclic forward, the disc tilts forward and the aircraft moves forward; push it back, the disc tilts back and the machine goes backwards.

'Take hold of the cyclic,' Graeme said. I did as instructed, feeling every vibration of the helicopter pass through my hand and up my arm. Graeme watched out of the corner of his eye, all the while keeping his hand on the dual cyclic.

'Don't choke it,' he said, observing my white-knuckled grip. 'This is how you do it.'

I looked over at Graeme. He was gently clasping the cyclic in between his fingers. I mimicked my instructor's technique. When he was satisfied, he handed me the cyclic. Instantly, we started to drift to the left. After my experience with the other instruments, I was careful not to overcompensate. I gently moved the cyclic right. Nothing happened. I moved it further to the right. The machine was still drifting.

'Hold her steady, please,' Graeme said.

I pushed the cyclic hard over to the right. We keeled over like a ship in a strong wind. Graeme took hold of the cyclic as the chopper continued moving to the right and quickly brought us back to an even plane.

'Try again,' he said.

The cyclic gave me a horrible time. It seemed to me that of all the controls, the chopper responded most sluggishly to the cyclic. It took me forever to stop the drift.

'Right,' Graeme said after my shambolic attempt to master the cyclic. 'Now that you know what each instrument is designed to do, I'm going to hand over control of the whole package.'

This is the reason Graeme Gillies is one of the best instructors going. Clearly, I wasn't ready to fly a helicopter. But Graeme believed in throwing his students in the deep end. It's only through trial and error that a person can learn how to fly a chopper. I completely understand why most instructors are reluctant to surrender control of the machine before they are certain the student is ready. Things can go badly wrong very quickly. But it means the whole process takes longer than necessary. Graeme had the confidence in his abilities to be able to regain control of a chopper, no matter the situation.

Graeme increased our altitude, most likely to increase the margin for error.

'The moment I think you're losing her,' he said, 'I'll take over.'

'Understood,' I said, with hands and feet at the ready.

'The controls are yours.'

In a flash, we were plunging towards the ground. Graeme took control immediately, returning us to altitude.

'Fucking hell!' he shouted. 'Small corrections.'

Once again Graeme handed me the controls and once again, I lost it. This time I overcompensated on the cyclic when I felt us drifting backwards and pitched our nose directly towards a building. Graeme guided us away without trouble.

For the rest of the lesson, Graeme handed me the controls for short periods. I'd generally be able to keep the chopper in a hover for about two seconds before the tail boom would suddenly drop down, or we'd yaw dangerously to the side, or we'd start spinning wildly on our axis. It was incredibly frustrating. I'd been accustomed to picking up the operation of machinery quickly. But this was entirely different.

To maintain the machine's centre of gravity, every action on one instrument required two simultaneous actions on two other instruments. It was like being the conductor of an orchestra, only you had to play every instrument yourself. Play one instrument too hard or another too soft and the machine would go out of harmony. It was a game of finesse, not force. And it was going to take a long time to get right.

'That's enough for today,' said Graeme. He took the controls and the chopper snapped into a stable position. He landed the helicopter and powered down. I sat quietly, waiting for an absolute bollocking.

'Well, that wasn't too terrible,' he said. 'Let's do the same thing tomorrow.'

* * *

It was a long process. Everything clicks one day; the chopper seems to be responding to every command and you fool yourself into thinking that you've got the whole thing under control. The next day rolls around and that magic touch has abandoned you, and the chopper is plunging, spinning and dipping out of control like on your first day at the controls.

Everyone wants to be an expert on the first go. Learning to fly a chopper isn't like that. There are no naturals. Flying a chopper is completely foreign. It takes hard work and dedication. The goal is to lay a foundation of understanding and build on it slowly. But not too slowly . . .

The initial down payment for the course covered me for 105 hours training. After racking up that many hours, I was eligible to go for a flying test to get my commercial licence. But there'd be no way Graeme would allow that to happen, not until I was completely proficient. The flying was tough, no doubt about it. But after four gruelling months I got it under control.

The theory component of my training was an altogether different headache. I'd never been much good at study. I was too restless to spend long stretches with my head in the books. I preferred the outdoors. I'd limped through my final school exams without spending a minute at home at the desk. This was going to be different. I'd staked my future and my fortune on being a helicopter pilot. Failure wasn't an option.

It took every ounce of concentration and discipline to keep me at the desk. Preparing for the seven exams was one of the hardest things I've ever done. It wasn't just a matter of learning the complexities of helicopter operations. I had to get across navigation, meteorology, air law and physics. I applied myself to the task like nothing before. I had no money so there was no drinking or partying anyway – distractions were minimal. I'd like to tell you that I passed those exams with flying colours. In fact, it was the opposite.

The major problem was that the Civil Aviation Safety Authority

(CASA) had contracted a New Zealand company to administer the exams. Not only were we all being prepared for a different model of examination, the tests were now conducted on computers. To make the whole thing 'more efficient', they crammed the exams into a short period of time. In the past it was one exam of three and a half hours; now we were doing seven exams in three days.

Everyone failed. Complaints were made but CASA wouldn't budge. We all had to retake the subjects from scratch. Another three months were lost. It was the worst possible outcome. I had no money to keep me flying with an instructor. I was absolutely livid. Instead of complaining, though, I directed all my energy into the books. I studied as if my life depended on it, because it did.

I remember walking back into the exam room for the first of my seven exams, almost shaking with nerves. If I didn't pass, I was going to have to consider bringing down the curtain on my dreams of flying. I couldn't afford to take another three months without work. Because the exam questions were multiple choice and taken on computer, the results were instantaneous. One by one, I finished off each exam through the week and blitzed every single one of them.

I remember celebrating with a couple of blokes at the end of that week. I couldn't wait to polish up my CV and start applying for work. That was until another chopper pilot and a great friend of mine, Michael Tweeds, gave me some advice.

'Matty, you want to get your ATPL,' he said, ATPL meaning Airline Transport Pilot Licence.

At the time I had gained a commercial helicopter licence, which was sufficient enough to do what I wanted. However, the ATPL would enable me to fly to oil rigs offshore with a larger number of passengers. It is a good retirement job but now was the time to do the theory behind it.

So I did. My grandmother agreed to stump up a few more thousand dollars to tide me over while I returned to the books and increased my flying time. It was a punishing three months, but by the end of it all I'd nailed my exams. On Graeme Gillies' recommendation, I applied for a job at North Australia Helicopters. I interviewed with chief pilot John Logan and he hired me on the spot. He was sending me to Moroak Cattle Station as a trainee mustering pilot. I've never been so excited. This was going to be the greatest experience of my life.

Before starting up at Moroak, I went home to see family and friends. I made sure to drop in on my schoolmate Phil Dickson, who was now learning how to fly choppers like his old man, Dave. Dave was thrilled for me when I told him that I was a qualified pilot. Several months earlier, Dave had finished building his experimental helicopter. He invited me to take it up for a spin. I jumped at the opportunity.

The design of Dave's helicopter was modelled on the old Bell series and included the distinctive bubble canopy. But Dave's chopper handled very differently. Not only were the controls sluggish, the whole machine vibrated and rattled in a worrying fashion. At that point, I had only piloted three different models of helicopter. I put my anxiety down to inexperience. After all, Dave's chopper was experimental. It was always going to feel different.

We landed without trouble and had a couple of beers together at Dave's place. With night falling, I headed back to Mum's place for dinner. It was the last time I saw Dave and Phil alive.

A month later, Dave took Phil up for a joyride in his helicopter. Witnesses to the accident described seeing bits of the machine falling apart before it fell out of the sky. The chopper speared into a shed and exploded on impact. Father and son were killed instantly. The coroner blamed the accident on a series of catastrophic mechanical failures. Dave left behind a wife and two daughters.

It was a terrible time. Dave's family lived in McLaren Vale and the whole community was in mourning. The accident shook me up, too. The instructors had drummed into us the dangers involved in flying helicopters and, as already mentioned, had been quick to point out that the majority of accidents are a result of pilot error. Dave and Phil's crash was a reminder that, when it comes to flying choppers, sometimes things just go horribly wrong.

10

Not a Job for
the Faint-Hearted

I hadn't met Milton Jones before I got to Moroak Station. I only knew him by reputation. Milton is a cult figure of the Northern Territory. He belongs to the old breed of station owner – those tough sons of bitches who are as rugged and hard as the land they work. He's a legendary cattleman, a highly successful business-man and one hell of mustering pilot.

Channel 10 made a show about him called *Keeping Up with the Joneses*. The show gave a glimpse of life on a cattle station and featured plenty of footage of helicopters mustering cattle and water buffalo. For extra drama, the producers decided to include a few scenes of Milton having some fun. Some scenes included Milton using his helicopter to tow his son across a lake on a wake-board, circling a watercourse while trying to bait a bull shark and hovering above a billabong while trying to snare a croc. CASA didn't like it one bit. Charges were laid and Milton was grounded until the matter was brought before court. This was the guy who was going to teach me how to become a mustering pilot!

Milton didn't even know my name for the first six months, or perhaps he did and he chose not to use it. He called me a lot of things but Matt wasn't one of them. I thought getting my licence was tough but working for Milton was hellish.

'Hey, you!' he'd bellow. 'Get over here!'

'Yes, Milton?'

'Go clean the shithouse.'

Off I'd go. It wasn't just cleaning toilets. Milton had me shoeing horses and mending fences like any old ringer. It was tough to be back on the menial jobs that I'd been doing on stations for years, but this is how it is for every mustering pilot. Nobody is put straight up in the chopper on day one. There were other things we had to master on Milton's station that were completely separate from learning how to become a mustering pilot. Top of the list was collecting crocodile eggs.

They say that fishing in the Bering Sea is the world's most hazardous occupation. The stats certainly back this claim. For every 100 000 crab-fishermen who brave those monstrous swells off the Alaskan coast, over 300 will drown or freeze to death. Nobody has died collecting crocodile eggs. The thing is, collecting croc eggs is a job beyond statistical comparison, because there are only about 15 people in the whole of Australia who do it. It's definitely not a job for everyone.

Here's some background on how egg collecting started. Between 1945 and 1971, an uncontrolled trade in saltwater crocodile skins depleted the wild population to the point of extinction. In 1971, the Territory government took action and enforced full protection of the species. By 1980, the base population had risen from 5000 to 30 000, which was an improvement but still nowhere near their original numbers, which is thought to have been around 100 000. Unfortunately, in the early 1980s, a string of crocodile attacks occurred, which threatened the conservation program. Many people were opposed to the further protection of the species. The public attitude towards crocs – an attitude that still persists in some sections of the community – was that these animals were monsters that should be culled.

This social upheaval led the Territory government to introduce a new strategy aimed at informing the public of the environmental and economic benefits of crocodile conservation. A key part of this strategy was egg collecting, which was and still is considered the safest way to encourage sustainable use and reward landowners for tolerating crocodiles on their properties. In 1987, Territory crocodile farms began exporting the skins produced from the harvested eggs they bought from landowners.

This incentive-driven wildlife practice has become the best conservation program in the world. Saltwater crocodiles are no longer a threatened species in the Territory, with over 140 000 in the wild. Frustratingly, there is still a lot of ignorance about egg collecting. People regularly lampoon egg collectors as greedy without understanding that it's part of a broader conservation strategy.

Now, onto how the egg collecting is done. Let me set the scene. You get slung into a swamp dangling from a chopper with sweat dripping from your forehead and clouding your vision. You land into what looks like a scene from *Jurassic Park*. It's 90 per cent humidity, 40-degree heat and there are spiders as big as your hands crawling up your trousers, leeches clinging to your arms, bull ants stinging your skin, deadly snakes slithering around your ankles and you can barely breathe through your gritted teeth as mosquitos fog the air.

But the worst is yet to come. You unhook from the chopper,

and your heart is racing as you know you've landed in croc country. The problem is, there is no croc to be seen. With one hand holding the crate for the eggs, you poke and prod the surrounding water with a six-foot pole for reassurance that it's safe to take another step forward. As you approach the croc nest, your senses are heightened. You're about to come face to face with the animal kingdom's number one predator – the saltwater crocodile.

I've been egg collecting for 15 years. Every nest has a different set of challenges. But if there's one constant challenge, it's definitely the crocodile that guards the nest. A crocodile – with its battery of senses, 180-degree field of vision, superior hunting ability, explosive speed and the strongest bite force of any animal on the planet – is not an animal to be treated lightly. You never know how big or aggressive the croc is going to be. All you can do is hope like hell that a big male isn't on guard of the nest. If you get caught napping, your little crate will be crunched like a Tic Tac and your pole will be used as a toothpick to clean up your remains.

Milton was all in favour of egg collecting. Not only was it a great way to keep the croc population on his station under control, there was also a financial incentive. I also got the feeling Milton enjoyed the job. After a lifetime spent working on cattle stations, Milton has probably seen it all. But collecting croc eggs is never boring. There are always different challenges and obstacles, because no nest is ever the same.

To begin with, there are lots of different areas that a croc will make a nest. There are nests built on floating grass, hidden in cane grass patches, nestling along rivers or billabong edges, situated on springs in the middle of salt flats and concealed in swamps. The only constant is that a female will build her nest in the vicinity of fresh water. Before laying her eggs, she will rake vegetation and leaf matter onto upturned logs or raised areas above the water line. Otherwise, she will build her nest in outcrops of cane and reeds. Water and reeds provide natural barriers around the nest and are also excellent places for the crocodile to stalk animals stupid or unfortunate enough to venture onto the nest.

When it came to mentors, I had some of the best. Milton would often bring along Bluey. Bluey was Milton's next-door neighbour. He was the owner of the Coolibah Crocodile Farm and knew all there was to know about crocs. I was learning from the best. Bluey showed me how to find the crocodile wallows – those burrowed-out depressions where crocs cooled off and waited in stealth. He would usually know the spot where the croc is most likely to attack from.

'Stay alert,' Bluey would say. 'Keep your eyes on the water.'

We'd leap onto the nest and start prodding the water around the nest with our poles. Once we'd established that the croc was nowhere to be seen, Bluey would set about collecting the eggs.

'Make sure you don't turn the eggs,' he said, carefully marking the egg with a pencil before gently placing it in the crate.

For an animal that grows into something so indestructible, a croc begins life as something very vulnerable. If you turn a crocodile egg on its axis, the yoke will crush and suffocate the embryo within. For that reason, they have to be packed in the crate in the upright position.

'If the eggs are packed properly,' Bluey would say. 'They'll survive.'

With all the manpower involved in collecting eggs plus the cost of running choppers all day, collecting eggs can be an expensive task. It's only viable if the collector returns with a good complement of eggs at the end of each day. A female lays anywhere between 30 and 80 eggs per season. A group of egg collectors will try to clear between 20 and 40 nests a day.

My first time collecting with Milton and Bluey is something I'll never forget. I was literally thrown into the deep end. Milton had just put Bluey on a nest and came back to pick me up. I jumped in the chopper and was ready with my stick and crate, quietly shitting myself. Being cramped in alongside Milton – who wasn't exactly a small lad – in an R22 was a reasonably uncomfortable experience. I was pretty eager to get out.

We flew into the jungle to an area called the 'vegie patch'. The ferns are about six feet tall, growing through a freshwater spring. Milton showed me the nest from the air and told me it was an easy one to get started on. He then zipped down and dropped me off. As he flew away, he told me to make sure I followed my same footsteps back out. Crocs move around beneath you through small channels. For this reason, it was important to jump from one fern bed to the next.

It was no easy task, but I felt I had everything under control. I was young, fit and raring to go. I bounced from one fern to the next until I reached the nest. I gave the nest a quick inspection and there was no croc to be found – happy days! I got all the eggs into the crate and headed back to the drop zone the best I could. Luckily, I managed to navigate back to the general area and in came Milton with the chopper. He hovered down next to me and I put the crate of eggs in a basket on the side of the chopper.

Just as I placed the crate of eggs I took one more step and lost my footing, disappearing down a hole into the water channel. Luckily my common sense prevailed and I didn't grab onto the chopper skid in panic. The R22 is a very light helicopter. Had

I reached out for the skid, the chopper and Milton would have tipped over and rolled into the swamp with me. I had no choice but to let myself fall into the water.

I slipped under the ferns and was there for what felt like ages. I tried to grab hold of firm ground, expecting a crocodile to take hold of my leg and pull me under. Eventually, I managed to claw myself back out and into the chopper. Milton assured me if there was a croc in that hole we would have known about it. It would have opened its mouth the moment he landed. Nevertheless, that mishap certainly got the blood rushing.

***

One of the great dangers of egg collectors doesn't come from the crocodiles. It comes from the searing heat. This was a lesson I learnt the hard way. Milton had dropped me off at the top of hill, high above a group of nests built on the banks of a river that snaked along the valley floor. I was given a set period of time to fill up the crate before I'd meet the chopper at a designated spot. I took off into the valley with a couple of water bottles and a crate for the eggs. It was piping hot. By mid-morning, the temperature was above 40 degrees and the humidity was high.

Compounding my discomfort was the location of the nests. They were burrowed deep in the cane grass. Crocs like building their nests in the cane grass because the tall, hard fronds provide excellent protection from predators. They grow up to three metres high and are nearly impossible to walk through. You have to push the grass over and crawl across it, which is incredibly taxing work. A lack of experience and youthful excitement resulted in me pushing myself too hard. Sure enough, after successfully clearing a couple of nests, I started to feel dizzy. Instead of taking it easy, I gulped down a bottle of water and shrugged it off. I was keen to get the job done before I met up with the chopper.

Less than an hour later I was spewing up my guts and shitting uncontrollably. Every time I tried to load up on water it came up before reaching my stomach. It felt like the inside of my body was on fire. I was suffering heat stroke and I still had a couple of hours before the chopper came back.

I found some shade and sat down, but it was no use. I needed to immerse myself in water. There were plenty of lagoons and lakes around, but none that you would want to enter. A dip in the croc-infested waters of the Northern Territory is suicide. The only other cool places I could think of were the crocodile wallows.

I'd seen an empty wallow near a nest I'd cleared earlier in the day. I backtracked along the bank of a lagoon, working hard to keep my balance. I could feel the energy seeping out of my body. I had to fight every instinct to sit down. When I finally came to the wallow, the owner had returned. She was dark in colour and about nine feet long. She was about to get very angry.

A crocodile, particularly a female during the nesting season, is fiercely territorial. In normal circumstances I would have kept my distance. The way I saw it, I had no choice. If I did nothing, I'd pass out and die. I was absolutely cooking and I still had a few more hours before the chopper was due to come and get me.

Cooling off in a wallow next to a croc might seem just as crazy as jumping into a croc-infested river. This was my rationale – if a crocodile bites you on land, bones will be crushed and lots of blood will be spilt; you may even lose a limb. But provided a major artery isn't severed or your head isn't ripped off, you stand a good chance of surviving. On the other hand, if a crocodile takes you into the water, there is no survival. You will be held under and violently rolled around until you drown. Find yourself in that scenario and your best outcome is a quick death.

I set my crate down in the shade of a tree and then, with pole in hand, walked over to the wallow. The croc kept utterly still. Flies buzzed around her head. She looked as if she was fast asleep. By now I'd been around crocodiles long enough to know better. She was completely aware of my presence. She was patiently waiting for me to walk into her strike zone before she'd leap at me, jaws snapping.

I took a wide berth around the wallow and approached from behind, remaining in the crocodile's blind spot. Once I was within striking distance, I took a deep breath, and gave her a big prod behind the back legs. She snapped around, ripping the pole from my grip and settled back into the pond. I now had no pole and no crate. Feeling as if I were about to faint at any moment, I went looking for another stick to cut down. I pulled my knife out and started hacking down a tree branch. Once I'd cut down the branch I was ready to go.

The battle resumed the moment I was back at the wallow. This time I went in with a little more determination. She tried yanking the stick from my hand again, but I managed to keep it out of her jaws. I moved her away from the wallow and then backed her up about 10 metres. Once she'd settled down, I returned to the wallow. Lowering myself into that cool water was an immense relief but it presented a new problem. With my body temperature lowering, I felt intensely fatigued. There was no way I could fall asleep. The crocodile never ventured more than 10 metres from that wallow. Every few minutes, she'd creep in too close for comfort. I would have to leap to my feet and move her again.

An hour or so had passed. I hauled myself out of the wallow, picked up my crate of eggs and plodded off down the valley to meet up with the chopper. Thankfully, the chopper arrived on time. After that I was bedridden for three days. My muscles screamed and I could barely hold down any food. Some of the boys thought I should have been sent to hospital and placed on a drip. I was in a bad way. Had it not been for that wallow, things might have ended up much worse.

11

The Big Cull

Before I became a mustering pilot, I first had to prove myself on the ground. That meant assisting the pilots on the bikes, horses and bull catchers. The country was tough to muster, especially around Roper River where Moroak was situated. A lot of the time we were chasing wild cattle, bulls and buffalo over huge distances. Often we would wait out on a flat area to help the mustering pilots as they pushed the herd into open country. Some of these paddocks were the size of capital cities, over 180 square kilometres of open country. They were long days. It was always a hard and fast round-up, but absolutely vital in terms of learning how to muster with the chopper. Milton said it best: 'To become a good mustering pilot, you've first got to understand cattle.'

After a couple of months, I started having a go on the dual controls with one of John Logan's veteran mustering pilots. Most of those blokes were happy to take me up. Sitting alongside a mustering pilot as he tossed his machine around ranks as one of the most exhilarating experiences of my life. The pilot would spear the chopper in towards the ground, bringing the skids and blades within inches of cattle in order to herd them towards the yard or a bull catcher. Countless times I thought we were going to collide with a tree or a gully or an animal. I'd be bracing for impact before the pilot would duck or weave away from trouble at the last moment. These guys were doing things with a helicopter that we'd been taught were impossible at flight school. The skill level was incredible. I couldn't wait to get started.

I had to wait most of the mustering season before I got my check flight with John. The check flight is the equivalent of a practical exam in which aspiring mustering pilots are set the relatively simple task of herding a mob of cattle into the house yard under the watchful gaze of an instructor. We were about two minutes into the muster when John shouted at me to put the chopper down. I was flying like a lunatic.

The rip-tear-bust attitude of the veteran pilots might be great to get a wild bull out of the jungle into the arm of a bull catcher, but putting a station owner's prize herd of cattle into the house yard required a gentler touch. He decided to move me down to our other base at Mount Isa, where I would muster on the Barkly Tableland. That way he could keep a closer eye on me.

John was a great mentor for junior pilots. He had over 15 000 hours' experience mustering cattle. But benefiting from the knowledge of one of the best in the business didn't make the task easy.

Helicopter mustering is one of the most demanding jobs in the aviation industry. Flying choppers is hard enough. But when you throw a couple of thousand head of cattle in the mix and the task of having to push them from one side of a paddock to the other in burning heat it becomes mentally taxing and physically fatiguing.

Most of the time you've got to stay high and fly slowly so the noise of the chopper moves the cattle along without causing stress.

Then there are times when you have to get the chopper close to the ground and move fast. For good reason, pilots call this flying in the dead-man zone. This is where things tend to go wrong.

When you're flying fast near the ground or around trees you have to maintain peak concentration to avoid a collision. While concentrating on not crashing, you also have to make sure the cattle are heading where you want them to go. John taught me that the mustering pilots to respect are those who fly without ego. Blokes who see themselves as cowboys of the sky are far more likely to end up dead. The job is about limiting risk, only pushing hard when absolutely necessary and always remembering that a human life is more important than a cow.

After a year under John's watch, I established a reputation as a reliable line pilot. I started getting moved around from station to station mustering cattle, buffalo and wild bulls. It was a great life. I had my own little R22 to look after with a rifle and swag on the passenger seat. This was why I got my chopper licence – it meant total freedom.

I'd fly from dawn to dusk to get the cattle to the yards and move on to the next station. If I ran out of daylight, I'd find a nice water hole where I'd roll out the swag near a fire and dream up my next adventure. Just like those days driving road trains through the emptiness of the Australian outback, I loved the non-conformity and being away from it all. There were, however, jobs I didn't like. Top of the list was culling feral animals, including pigs, water buffalo, wild horses, donkeys, camels, goats, and deer. But nothing was worse than culling brumbies.

Mobs of brumbies or wild horses have been roaming the Australian countryside since the beginning of European settlement. At present, there are approximately 400 000 brumbies in the Australian wild. Traditionally located in the Australian Alps of Victoria and New South Wales, large numbers can be found in the Northern Territory and Queensland. They comprise a variety of breeds, including Timor ponies, draught horses, Arabians, thoroughbreds and 'capers' from South Africa. Escaped farm horses and discarded army horses often join a mob, adding to the diversity of breeds. With their hard hooves horses erode soil, trample vegetation, and damage bog and waterhole habitats. They chew bark off trunks resulting in widespread destruction of native tree species and also spread invasive weeds.

Brumbies are also a nightmare for farmers. They destroy farm infrastructure, such as fences, pipes and water troughs. They dig up grazing ground for cattle. Although not nearly as damaging to the ecosystem as other introduced species like rabbits, cane toads, wild pigs and foxes, brumbies have been listed as a pest by government officials and environmentalists for decades. They need to be dealt with, which is easier said than done.

Anyone who has had to shoot a wild horse will tell you that it's a heartbreaking job. Most ringers and stockmen grew up on farms. They have been around horses all their lives and developed a special affinity for this beautiful animal. Blokes who have taken part in big brumby culls will admit to suffering nightmares for months. I've even seen grown men break down and cry after shooting a horse. Watching brumbies run free across the outback is among the most beautiful things you will see in the wild. No matter the justification, shooting them feels immoral. I had always managed to avoid jobs that involved horse culls until a station owner tasked me with a job that would change my life forever.

It happened on a station in far north Queensland. The station manager wanted my help in dealing with a dingo problem. Packs of dingoes were attacking the station's young cattle. Calves would get their ears ripped off, their soft underbellies torn open or backs eaten out. A cheap way of managing this problem in the Top End is dropping from a helicopter or plane a haunch of meat doused in 1080 – a cheap pesticide that in large doses brings about a metabolic poisoning in dingoes. The station was enormous, over a million acres. That meant a lot of meat was needed. By the time I arrived, the station manager had come up with a tidy solution.

'What I'll get you to do,' he said, 'is fly me out and I'll shoot some horses.'

My heart sank. The station manager went on to explain that his property was overrun with brumbies. Reducing their numbers while providing the meat needed for the dingo problem was a good way of killing two birds with one stone.

'Are you a good shot?' I asked.

'I'm a great shot,' he said.

I had my doubts. Hitting a moving target from a hovering helicopter is not easy. But there was no talking him out of it. This bloke was all keyed up for a hunt and I was employed to do a job. I powered up the R22 and off we went.

It took us no time to find a mob of 10 brumbies. They were grazing in open country. This was good. I'd be able to take the chopper in low without having to skirt around trees. If the station owner was as good a shot as he claimed, he should be able to take down a couple of horses without trouble.

The mob bolted as I brought the chopper in close. The brumbies all got in behind the stallion – a beautiful chestnut Waler. The Waler has a long association with the Australian military. In earlier conflicts, particularly the Boer War and the First World War, the Waler was the most sought-after breed among Australian

Light Horse units. Hardy and tough, the Waler performed superbly in the deserts of North Africa and the open plains of South Africa. It goes just as well in the Australian outback. These days the army maintains Walers for ceremonial duties.

I took the chopper down and ran alongside the big stallion while the station manager lined him up. As he squeezed off a couple of rounds, I felt sick in the guts. Shooting from a chopper at a proud stallion felt completely wrong. It got worse when I saw the stallion buck in agony as the bullets punched into him. I could see blood pouring out of bullet holes in his neck and withers. But this was a strong animal. Only a kill shot would bring him down.

'Shoot him in the head!' I shouted.

'I'm trying!'

As I feared, the station manager was not such a hot shot after all. He put another five bullets into the poor animal, but failed to bring him down. I decided to pull up.

'What are you doing?' shouted the station owner.

'I've got a better idea.'

I scouted the terrain below and found a narrow ravine. I set the chopper down nearby and laid out my plan.

'Wait here,' I said. 'I'll run these horses up and you shoot them when they come past.'

He nodded his head enthusiastically. Once the station manager was out of the chopper, I took off and headed back to the field where I'd left the horses. I found the mob bunched around the stallion. He was hopping around, blood seeping out of his wounds. I set the chopper down nearby, dispersing all the horses. The stallion could barely manage a canter. I took out my pistol, walked up to him and put a bullet in his head. He crumpled to the ground dead. It was devastating.

The rest of the horses had gone off in all directions when they heard the gunshot. I ran back to the chopper and got airborne. I rounded them up and guided them towards the ravine. They bunched in tightly together, just as I hoped. In the distance, the station manager had his rifle raised, waiting for the herd. I doubted that this bloke had the skill to bring down nine charging horses. There was no way I was going to condemn these animals to the same fate as the stallion. I was going to make sure these horses were down before that happened.

I pulled up and circled around the horses. The horses skidded to a halt before changing direction. I dropped in low beside them and started picking them off one-by-one. Once the last horse fell, I set the chopper down and went to inspect the horses. I wanted to make sure none of them were still alive or in pain. The station manager came bounding up.

'I had them covered,' he said. 'You didn't need to do that.'

I wanted to tell him that he wasn't a good enough shot to give these animals a clean kill. But there was no need. He got the message. He radioed his boys back at the homestead and gave them our position. About 10 minutes later, several blokes in a couple of land cruisers rolled out to our position.

As I watched the boys butcher up the meat, I couldn't believe the waste. All of these horses could have been herded back to the yard and broken in. It's true that in the motorised age cattle stations no longer depend on horses like they once did. But these horses could easily have been sold interstate or internationally. Anything was better than killing them for dingo bait.

I went to bed that night, haunted by what I had just done. At some point an idea popped into my head. If everyone was against the idea of culling brumbies, why was it still going on?

The key was getting the message out to people in the big smoke and attempting to put an economic value on our feral animals in Australa. I wasn't interested in some boring old news report. I wanted to do something bigger.

Looking back, I reckon that was the point the idea of a television show took hold. I didn't act straight away, partly because I didn't know where to start. But I never let go of the dream. So when the opportunity to get something going presented itself, the idea for what I wanted to do was clear in my mind. In the end, my big break came on another hard day's work. It happened a couple of years after the brumby episode while I was working on one of the toughest cattle stations in Australia – Wrotham Park.

12

Murder in the Outback

Situated in far north Queensland, Wrotham Park Station is 600 000 hectares of limestone escarpments, towering rocky pillars, rainforest country, rivers, billabongs and rolling hills. It's beautiful country, ideal for grazing while offering cattle plenty of places to cool off in the shade. It's also a nightmare for a mustering pilot and not just because of the terrain.

I'd been sitting up in Mount Isa when the call came through to John Logan. One of the other pilots, a bloke by the name of Nick, had been in a bad crash. They needed someone to sling what remained of Nick's chopper back to the homestead. Witnesses to the crash said that he was pushing the cattle in towards the yard when he was hit by a microburst – a sudden downdraft that occurs in thunderstorms and is lethal to low-flying aircraft. The chopper nearly flipped on its lid. He overcompensated, pulling the cyclic back too hard and putting the main rotor back through his tail boom. He levelled out and for a split second everything seemed fine, but the damage to the tail boom was catastrophic. It snapped off. Without the anti-torque rotor, the helicopter went into a violent spin, flipped onto its side and barrel-rolled several times before miraculously landing upright. He was dragged out unconscious suffering only a broken arm from the main rotor blade coming down through the cab of the chopper. He was lucky to have survived.

I ended up taking over from him at Wrotham Park. It would have been better if Nick retired then. He instead decided to get back up in the air and flew for another few years as a mustering pilot at other stations around Australia. He put a few more machines into the ground along the way. He met his end out on a dual muster due to a fault in the machine.

Wrotham Park was infamous for chopper crashes. Prior to my time, several pilots mustered that country and crashed regularly. One bloke crashed nine times and the lucky bastard still managed to survive. I even remember back to when I was doing my licence I was always hearing stories of Wrotham Park. The cattle were wild and its rubber-vine jungles were treacherous. This was not a place to be treated lightly.

A big part of mustering on Wrotham Park involved catching cleanskin cattle. We call them cleanskins because they have never been brought to the yard. As such, these animals have unblemished skin having never been branded or earmarked. They are bred in the wild and grow up that way, charging anyone who dares to come near.

Cleanskins are worth a bit, provided you can get them into the yard without wasting resources or getting yourself killed. If a bull is too dangerous, then it has to be shot. I did a bit of bull catching with Milton at Moroak and Coolibah. It was great fun, heading out on bull catchers, bikes or horseback and head-roping a big old wild bull. But at Wrotham Park there was a higher degree of difficulty.

The cattle up in that corner of the country are ferocious. Every worker who has set foot on Wrotham Park has a story about being hit by wild cattle. I was smoked a few times myself. Often it was the little ones that caused you the most grief. Like the one that nearly did me in while I was bull catching with my great mate Brett Wild.

'Wildy' was always good to go bull catching with. He was cool, calm and collected and had worked his way up through the ranks to become head stockman. One day we came across an unassuming little red bull. This was an easy get. When he saw us coming, he turned round and bolted. I gave my horse a kick and went after him. The little bull took me through an outcrop of eucalyptus trees. I ducked under low-hanging branches and hung on for dear life as my horse cleared fallen timber and boulders. This little fella was giving us a good run around.

Once I was out of the trees and onto an open plain, I had him. I brought the horse right up behind him and then dismounted, running hard as I hit the ground with a rope slung over my shoulder. I reached out to grab his tail when the little bastard turned round and sideswiped me. It was a perfectly timed hit. I ended up landing face first in the dirt. Luckily, the bull's horns were only small. I put my arms over my head to protect myself against serious injury as he came at me. He got his little horns under me lifting me up and rolling me round for about a minute. Wildy was roaring with laughter.

'Wildy' I shouted. 'Give me a hand!'

He dismounted and ran up behind the bull and grabbed his tail. The bull kicked and bucked violently, managing to free himself from Wildy's grip. Now it was my turn to do the laughing as Wildy was chased round and round a tree. He had left his rope on the horse and had nowhere to hide. I dusted myself off and ran back in to help out. For such a small bull he had a heck of a lot of go in him. After 15 minutes, we eventually managed to wrestle him down to a creek bed where we were able to hold him down, get a head rope on him and tie him to a tree to cool down.

The problem with little bulls is that they tend to have greater stamina. Although big bulls are significantly more dangerous, they are usually easier to catch. The trick with the bigger bulls is to get right up on them as fast as you can and puff them out. This means you have to push them as hard and fast as you can in a very short distance so they tire quickly. When the bull slows down to catch his breath, you jump off your bike and grab hold of his tail. Then you run forward and just as he tries to spin you pull him down. If you're quick enough this usually works. If you're too slow then you have to find yourself a tree to hide behind. As the bull charges you throw your catching rope around his horns and tie him up to the tree. In theory, this seems simple enough. In practice, it can be a very different story.

* * *

I was out catching a few bulls with my mate Sam Alford. Sam loaned me his dirt bike while he went on horseback. We spotted a big old cleanskin drinking from the bank of a creek. I gave the bike full throttle and was up alongside him in no time. He seemed a pretty relaxed old boy. That was until I drew up next to him on the bike. This big old fella had a huge spread of horns that tapered off into sharp ends. I got a great pump on him through the thick riverside shrub, or so I thought . . .

I jumped off the bike and managed to get the stand down so the bike didn't topple over. I ran flat out towards the bull and reached out for his tail just as he spun around on me like a ballerina. Standing at arm's length with the bull, I noticed just how lethally sharp the ends of his horns were.

I put my hand out on his forehead and hazed him off as I ran backwards looking for a tree to get behind. There wasn't much around, so I got behind the bike. I ran the bull round and round in circles, using the bike as a barrier. The bull was getting increasingly frustrated. Rather than run around the bike, he decided to get it out of the way. He dropped his head, and stuck one horn through the back tyre and one through the fuel tank. He lifted the bike in the air and walked off.

Sam arrived at that very moment.

'What the hell is he doing with my bike?' he shouted.

The bull took off back down towards the river with the bike stuck to his horns. It was a pretty funny sight, although Sam wasn't laughing. We gave chase, mainly to get the bike back. The bull eventually dropped the bike and then disappeared into some pretty tough country. Considering a bull had just impaled it, I thought the bike looked in pretty good condition. Sam didn't agree. I didn't hear the end of that one!

Those were memorable run-ins with wild cattle, but they weren't life-threatening. When a fully grown wild bull comes at you, it's no laughing matter. A mate of mine named Dallas Steele was out catching bulls at the Park. He found an enormous cleanskin, and got him to a tree. Round and round they went till the bull got the better of him. The bull put one of his horns right through Dallas' stomach. He lifted him up and carried him for about 15 metres before dumping him on the ground. Dallas survived, the horn missing vital organs by a matter of centimetres.

I've had a couple of good episodes with cranky bulls. They're not times I'll easily forget. A couple of boys had come across a cleanskin that was way too tough to haul back to the yard. They chased him on horseback and put six bullets into him. The bull was a hardy old bastard and managed to escape. I was told to get up in the R22 and go finish off the job. Before I left, the head stockman gave me a warning.

'There's nothing more dangerous than a wounded bull,' he said.

I nodded my head and took off in the chopper. I found the bull lying in the shade of a tree in a creek bed. From the sky, he looked to be dead. But I wasn't taking any chances. After setting the chopper down, I drew my pistol and carefully approached on foot. The bull was slumped over. He didn't look to be breathing. The only sign of life was the blood pumping out of his bullet wounds. I got to within two metres when the bull pulled himself up. He lifted his head and eyeballed me. I'll never forget the look of madness in those eyes. He meant to kill. I registered one thought at the moment: *Oh shit!*

The bull stood up. I took a couple of steps backwards, never lowering my gun. I wasn't going to fire unless necessary. If I shot the bull and didn't kill him, the damn thing would certainly charge me.

I made my way behind an old rotten tree trunk. It was about the thickness of a man's leg. Once I was safely behind the trunk, the bull charged. I had a round of six bullets. I squeezed off two shots, the bullets literally bouncing off his hard head and stirring him up even more. The bull burst through the rotten log as if it was made out of cardboard. He lowered his head, intent on goring me with his horns. The move exposed the top of his head. The bull was now inches away from ramming me. In that final split second, I put the gun against his head and pulled the trigger. I remember the clicking sound of the gun jamming before everything went black.

The next thing I remember was waking up completely disoriented. The bull had thrown me 20 feet. Fortunately, I was wearing my helicopter helmet. But I didn't get away scot-free. When I tried to move I felt incredible pain in both my arms. I looked down to see the sleeves of my shirt drenched in blood. The bull had put a hole in each arm.

I got to my feet and staggered over to the chopper. Luckily, the bull was nowhere to be seen. I flew back to the house and got patched up. It could have been a lot worse.

* * *

During my time at Wrotham Park, I did some contract mustering to the neighbouring cattle stations, including Bolwarra, Blackdown, Bulimba and Mount Mulgrave. Some of these places are so remote that you can inhabit a world of your own without too much outside contact. As such, they are the perfect sorts of places to engage in crime.

Take, for example, the story of chopper pilot Peter Pantovic. A couple of mates of mine, brothers Tony and Greg Hicks, bought Bolwarra Station from Pantovic back in 2005. The station was located southwest of Chillagoe in Queensland. It looked like a promising business venture. The two brothers couldn't have known that they were stepping into the underworld.

Alarm bells probably should've started ringing when Pantovic agreed to sell the station on the proviso that he could remain as a mustering pilot. It turned out Pantovic had teamed up with drug kingpin Alexander Malcolm Lane and was running a hefty operation on the backblocks of Bolwarra.

After a year or so, the Hicks boys didn't like having Pantovic around. For one thing, they felt he was a substandard mustering pilot. So they called me in and I ended up doing a lot of work around the station. I mustered the station for over two years but never flew over the backblocks because it was bad country with no cattle.

Even though Pantovic finished up mustering he continued to work with Lane and three other members to continue the multi-million-dollar syndicate. The size of the station was so vast, they could use helicopters to ferry men and supplies into the remote bush camps without the Hicks boys realising what was happening on their property. Pantovic and his goons grew tonnes of high-grade cannabis every year, earning up to $300 000 each crop, which was reportedly paid in cash and gold bullion. There was so much money coming in, the syndicate bosses had to bury it in secret caches, including down a mineshaft.

I'll never forget the day I woke up with chopper pilots calling me all morning asking if I knew about the bust at Bolwarra. I had no idea what was going on. The police had raided the station after receiving a tip-off. An aerial search of the property revealed an empty chopper. The chopper was still running with no pilot. A manhunt began immediately. Police called me and every other mustering pilot in the area. All of us were under investigation until the police busted Pantovic. In 2007, Pantovic, Lane and the other syndicate members were sentenced after a three-year joint police and Australian Crime Commission investigation traced the syndicate across Australia and to Europe. It would go down as one of Australia's most sophisticated marijuana growing cartels.

I got the call up from the Hicks brothers after the police had finished with the site. The coppers had told the Hicks boys that they could have what was left of the camp infrastructure the syndicate had set up. So I flew out with the boys. Flying out there, we were all waiting in anticipation to see what this camp was like and, bloody hell, you could see it from a mile off. With all of the nutrients that had been pumped into the ground the valley in which the camps were set up looked like a lush oasis in the middle of the desert. We landed in the valley where we saw cleared areas with an army-like camp set-up.

The cops did a reasonable job of cleaning the place out for evidence but as we explored further we came across harvested crops of dope piled up over six feet tall. I'd never seen anything like it. The cops had tried to burn it but there was so much there it hadn't burnt all the way through. We set it in on fire and kept searching the camp for useful remnants. I hooked up tents, gas fridges, irrigation systems and Cryovac machines and flew them back to the house.

On the way back, I couldn't get over what I had just seen. Nor could I believe the scale of the operation that was operating under our noses for so long. It says a lot about the vastness of the Australian outback.

* * *

After Pantovic was locked up I got some more work at a station he used to muster north of Wrotham Park called Palmerville Station. Palmerville was located near Maytown in the centre of the Palmer River goldfields. The region enjoyed a boom between 1873 and 1890, recording a total output of gold of more than 15 500 kilograms. But those years were a distant memory. Although there were still operating gold mines around the property, the gold yield was relatively small. That didn't stop the prospectors turning up looking to make it rich.

Steve Struber, the owner of Palmerville Station, hated the roaming prospectors coming onto his land. He had no choice but to tolerate their presence because of their mining leases. Once every few months Steve would call me up to muster his wild bullocks, which were a handful to get into the yards. I soon learnt that Steve had no idea how to muster cattle or run a station. I ended up taking the lead and gave him a hand to set things up properly.

My mates Luke and Leon Kingsley, who owned the neighbouring station Mount Mulgrave, used to give me shit for working for Struber. They thought he was as mad as a cut snake. I didn't mind the bloke. We got on okay and he paid well. But I didn't know much about his personal life. That is until the day I mustered with his wife Di. She had asked to come with me in the chopper to help spot the cattle. I guess it was a bit out of the blue, but I didn't think much of it at the time.

I noticed that Di seemed a little bit jumpy. It didn't take long to work out why. Once we got airborne, she told me that Steve was beating on her and was afraid he was going to kill her. I was in shock. I kept her in the chopper so she could calm down and we finished the job together. Before I dropped her off, I told her she should leave Steve. She shook her head and told me not to tell anyone. I felt sick in my guts when I flew home that night. I called Steve the next day and told him I wouldn't be coming back. It seemed the Kingsley boys were right. Steve Struber was crazy. It turned out he was crazier than anyone expected.

I was sitting on the couch just the other day watching *A Current*

Affair when the name Steve Struber came up. The story concerned a law that was being passed that prevented the release of convicted murderers from jail even if they have served their sentences, unless they disclosed the whereabouts of their victim's body. Strike me dead, up pops a picture of Stephen and Dianne Struber. It turned out they were both sentenced to life behind bars in 2015 for slaying a gold prospector named Bruce Schuler. They found Schuler fossicking up a dry gully on Palmerville Station. The body still hasn't been found and they won't 'fess up as to its location. I spent the night reflecting on that wild time in my life, working with the dark characters of the Aussie outback.

13

The Big Round-Up

The station owner at Wrotham Park pulled me into his office. It was the morning of the second day of a huge round-up. We were mustering 4000 head of cattle several kilometres over two days. It was one of the largest paddocks on the property – we had flown from daylight to dark to get just half the paddock mustered. It was a big day with four choppers in the air constantly ducking and weaving in and out of the river and trees to get the cattle out onto the flat for Wildy and his crew. This is called coach mustering. All the bikes and horses hold the mob of cattle while the choppers go wide and bring in more. It saves the chopper pilots having to keep track of the whole herd of cattle. Not only is coach mustering more efficient, it has the added bonus of educating the cattle at the same time.

We'd flown 10 hours straight – about twice the normal flying time required for a day in the sky – just to get them into a temporary holding yard. The yard was set up near the Mitchell River, a big river that snakes through the station. The plan was to let the cattle have a small drink at first light then march them to the main yard. It was going to be another big one, but I was confident we had things under control. The boss was about to throw a spanner in the works.

'R.M. Williams are coming up today to do a photo shoot,' he said. 'You'll need to fly a photographer around a bit to take a few photos.'

'No problem,' I said. 'I'll do it after we get the cattle up to the fence line.'

Once a mob of cattle is at the fence line, the hard work is done. The land cruisers and quad bikes can push them up into the yard.

'Matty,' he said, grinning. 'They want to take photos of you.'

The General Manager of Marketing and Sales, Arabella Gibson, wanted to get a few shots of a mustering pilot wearing their gear. It was fine by me. Not only would I get paid, I'd also get to keep the boots and clothes. We agreed to shoot the following day after the morning's muster.

It was a camped cooked brekky to start the day – steak and eggs with a strong black coffee. Then it was all hands to the wheel. It was still dark as the stockmen were getting their horses and bikes ready. I was doing the daily look over the chopper and getting it filled up. We had three machines in the sky and worked them hard that day, desperate not to let any bulls slip away. It took us about eight hours, but eventually we had cleaned out the river and pushed most of the cattle right up to the fence line.

I flew directly to the Wrotham Park Resort and left one chopper there keeping an eye on things. There were a few models sitting around talking to Arabella. They were getting ready for an afternoon shoot when the setting sun transforms the landscape into its most photogenic state.

I introduced myself to Arabella. Then I took the photographer up for a few shots of me piloting the chopper. I set the helicopter down near the cattle and posed for the camera, leaning up against the front of the R22 with the cattle in the background. The boys on the ground were all having a good laugh at my expense. I felt like a bit of dickhead. Soon enough, I would have more important things to worry about.

One by one, cattle that were slowly being worked up the fence line started peeling back. The bikes and horsemen were having difficulty keeping them on the fence. I immediately got my machine up in the air. There were only a couple dozen that were going the wrong way. I figured I'd have no trouble rounding them up.

Suddenly, a couple dozen more turned around, then a dozen more, and a dozen after that. On it went. Before long, there were hundreds streaming past. It was late in the afternoon. These animals were in need of a drink. Obviously there was water up in the holding paddock where we intended to keep them overnight, but they weren't to know that. As far as these cattle were concerned, the nearest drinking spot was all the way back at the river.

Other than myself, there was one other chopper handy. I had let the other two blokes knock off early thinking the bulk of the work had been done. I got on the radio to base straight away and told them to get those two boys airborne. I left the photographer in one of the LandCruisers. There was no way of getting him back to the resort. I couldn't spare any of those vehicles. He was going to be with us for the rest of the day. Not that he minded. He was a freelancer and he was getting some terrific shots of the choppers doing their best to round up the stampeding cattle.

The guys working for R.M. Williams were a different story.

I started getting radioed every half hour wanting to know what was happening with their photographer.

'He'll be back when we're finished out here,' I said.

'When will that be?'

I felt like telling them to go and jam it. Instead, I told them I'd get him back soon just to get them off my back.

It was five o'clock. We had less than two hours of light. The mob had scattered as far as the eye could see. After about an hour of pushing harder than ever, we got them along the fence line. They were strung out over five kilometres. At the very limit of the horizon, all you could see was cattle. Using the fence as a barrier, the choppers, horsemen, bikes and vehicles hustled them up towards the cooler.

Night had fallen by the time they were all penned in. I'd flown close to 20 hours over a couple of days. That's a huge amount of time in the air in a helicopter. But the job still wasn't done. The cattle were stirred up, with the headstrong bulls trying to push back through the wire fence. The only way to keep them from stampeding was to power up all four choppers and leave them running with the lights on for over an hour while the cattle calmed down.

The R. M. Williams crew was not impressed. They would have to spend another day out at the resort. But Arabella was happy with the snaps the photographer took. While I was enjoying a well-earned beer with the boys, she approached with the offer to do more modelling work.

'Why not?' I asked.

You can imagine the response from the boys. They were clutching at their sides with laughter. Working on a cattle station draws the kind of bloke who eats red meat and drinks beer. It's not exactly the place for a model. Truth be told, I wasn't interested in modelling. I had my sights set on TV.

* * *

For a long time, the idea of putting together a television show that gave a glimpse of life in the Australian outback had been building in my mind. I had the stories, the experience and the will. What I didn't have was contacts in the Australian media and entertainment world. Arabella was the kind of person who knew people who might help get my stuff broadcast. But before I started introducing myself to producers and network executives, I needed to show them my stuff.

Every opportunity I got, I would have my handy camera out filming. Everyone got roped in to help me out, from the resort's head chef to the young jackaroos that came to the park for an adventure. I'd offer them a free flight in the chopper on the proviso they held the camera. Otherwise, I'd be nagging girlfriends or mates to film me catching snakes, catching bulls on horseback, breaking in a brumby or poking a croc with a stick. The boys gave me heaps of shit. But I didn't care. I'd become determined to get a show going.

Every weekend I'd fly into Cairns and stay with mates. I'd rent out an editing suite and get to work. The footage was very amateurish: shaky and hard to watch. A lot of the time, entire sequences were out of focus. Even worse, I'd be talking but slipping out of the frame!

The better stuff was the selfie footage where I had set my camera up on a rock. It was the only material you could watch without laughing. I'd film myself with a snake or just doing a piece to camera, talking about life in the Top End. The footage is pretty cringe-worthy. There's no excitement in my voice at all and I walk around as if I have a stick up my arse. Even while I was editing it I knew it was rough. But I managed to get a bit of interest from the networks thanks to Arabella, who provided introductions. They offered to buy them for bottom dollar and then broadcast them as clips on the morning shows.

Making it in television is tough. Most of the time, I got knocked back. I started to lose more money than I was making. After two years, I decided to pack it in. Australian Agriculture Company decided to sell Wrotham Park to Great Southern, another massive beef cattle producer. New management came in and everything changed. It felt like a good time for a new adventure.

By now, I'd racked up about 4000 hours as a mustering pilot. I was starting to get a bit tired of chasing cows around paddocks. I wanted to try a different type of flying in a different type of helicopter. A few mustering pilots had talked to me about getting work over in Canada. The money was twice as good and the flying was said to be insane. I had a bit of money saved up, and nothing tying me to Australia, so why not?

At the end of the egg-collecting season in February, I jumped on a plane and flew across the Pacific. It was the start of one of the greatest experiences of my life.

14

Canada

I travelled up to Abbotsford in British Columbia to sit my conversion test. I passed without too much hassle and received my Canadian helicopter licence. I had no trouble finding employment, landing a job with the first helicopter business I applied to. The name of the company was Qwest Helicopters.

Qwest was run by a couple of veteran chopper pilots and was operated out of Fort Nelson and Fort St John. The company had a long tradition of service in northern British Columbia; most of their flying was for the oil patch and forestry. There was also aerial firefighting, medevac, VIP transport and work up in the mountains.

I loved the job from the get-go. I did heaps of hours and the coin was good. Most of all, the flying was brilliant. This was a far cry from the mainly flat, sun-parched red country of the Australian north. Now I was flying alongside towering cliff faces, snowy mountaintops and dramatic escarpments. I was suddenly faced with a whole set of different challenges. With snowstorms whipping up in a flash, there was the constant threat of being caught in a white out. I was also flying at much higher altitude, where a helicopter's rotors struggle to maintain lift in the thinner air. It was my lack of experience flying at in these conditions that played a part in my first and only crash in a helicopter.

I was taking a group of surveyors north of Fort Nelson. They were conducting oil and gas exploration for a major company. Working with Canada's primary industries was a mainstay for Qwest and this was going to be a big job. I flew out in the company's Bell 206, the Jet Ranger. With a reputation for safety and reliability, the Jet Ranger has been popular among pilots since it was first rolled out in the 1960s. I had a complement of four passengers with the plan to find a firm patch of ground to drop three of them off and take one back up the hill to jump out of the chopper and cut a pad for me to land. Then I would go back and get the remaining crew so they didn't have to walk for miles knee deep in snow.

I found a spot to land at the intersection of two seismic lines. A seismic line is a bulldozed pathway through forest, allowing a passage for drills, equipment and power cables to be laid. Even though it was late in the summer, the seismic lines were carpeted with snow and ice. From above, it looked to be firm ground. I was about to learn that when it comes to finding firm ground on which to land in northern Canada, looks can be deceiving.

My approach to the intersection of the seismic lines was very smooth. I set her down without much drama. We sat there for a few minutes; I held power on while the crew decided what they wanted to do. Plans changed and they agreed they were going to walk up to the surveyed area and conduct their work. I lowered the collective and wound the throttle back to idle. That's when things went wrong.

Within seconds I felt the machine rock backwards on the right-hand side. I tried to wind the throttle back and get out of there but the turbine wasn't responsive. The chopper dropped further backwards and the tail hit the ice. The machine started to shake violently so I shut it down and held the cyclic forward keeping the main rotor away from the ice. I knew if the rotor hit the ice it would have been catastrophic. The gearbox would have ripped off the machine, sending the body of the chopper into a violent spin and leaving us cactus. One of the young women in the back of the chopper started screaming. She really lost it.

'We're going to die! We're going to die!' she screamed.

I told her to shut up while I tried to work out what to do. We all watched with mounting dread as the rotor inched closer and closer to the ice.

'Let me out!' The woman screamed, tears streaming down her eyes.

'Sit down,' I said, firmly. 'Everyone is going to be fine.'

The machine dropped suddenly again, bringing the rotor to within about a foot of the ice. To compensate, I held the cyclic full over to the left. The whole machine started to shudder and groan. The chopper was fighting hard to stay above the ground. It felt like hours before that helicopter powered down fully and the rotor stopped spinning.

I gave the all clear for everyone to slowly exit the chopper. Everyone piled out at lightning speed. I was worried that a sudden weight variance might cause the helicopter to sink further. But she remained steady. Once everyone was out I inspected the inside of the helicopter. Water had flooded into the back, saturating a couple of bags, including my own. My laptop was destroyed. Otherwise everything was okay.

My major concern was exterior damage. If the tail rotor was damaged the cost of repair would be enormous. I walked around the back of the aircraft with my heart in my mouth. Luckily, when the skid broke through the ice, the chopper fell back towards the right. The tail rotor is located on the left side of the tail boom. Aside from a bit of a dent at the back of the chopper, the machine appeared to be undamaged. Now all I had to do was work out how to get it out of the icy water. I turned to the passengers.

'You guys get on with your work,' I said. 'I'll get on the radio and sort this out with the guys back at base.'

Off they went, convinced I had the situation under control. Nothing could have been further from the truth.

The radio was undamaged, but we had flown a long way from base. We were beyond range. There was always the unappealing option of activating the EPIRB (Emergency Position-Indicating Radio Beacon). Turning on an EPIRB is not something done lightly. The huge cost involved in dispatching every rescue helicopter and plane not to mention search parties often results in public enquires. The last thing I wanted was to risk losing my licence. It would also result in Qwest suffering devastating reputational damage.

The other option was to wait for Qwest to send someone up to find me. Base was expecting me back within an hour. If I didn't turn up, they would attempt to hail me on radio. When that failed, they would send a couple of choppers out to go look. It was hard to imagine that they wouldn't spot me. But it was still a risk. If they failed to locate us, we would face a night sleeping rough in sub-zero temperatures. That was a risk I wasn't prepared to take. But just before I activated the EPIRB, an idea popped into my head. I remembered one of the other pilots was on a job nearby. She might just be in radio range. It was worth a try. I got on the radio.

'Tara, this is Matty. Do you copy?' I asked.

'Loud and clear, Matty,' she said.

I breathed a sigh of relief. I told her that I'd been involved in a little incident and needed her advice. I gave her my coordinates and she was overhead within a couple of minutes.

'How do I look from up there?' I asked.

'I don't think you are getting out in a hurry.'

'Listen, can you radio base for me?'

'What do you want me to say?'

'Just tell them I've had a minor accident. Make sure you tell them that nobody has been hurt and the helicopter is intact.'

'Okay,' she said. 'Anything else?'

'We'll need another chopper, some rigging gear and an empty fuel drum.'

'No worries, Matt. I'll get it sorted. I'd tell ya to have a good day but it looks like it's started off pretty bad.'

Tara radioed base. The boss sent out Mike Koloff to fix the problem. Mike was the company's training pilot and one of the best sling pilots going round. He was regularly called on by the local fire department to sling water onto the raging wildfires Canada experiences in the summer months.

The company's engineer, Cory Hoover, came too, along with the boss, Zvonko Dancevic. Zonk, as we called him, was a veteran pilot who started Qwest up with his mate Cam Allan. He was seriously pissed off when he arrived. He had good reason to be. One of his choppers was in the water. If it stayed there overnight, it would have frozen. There were also big chunks of ice floating in the water. The longer the chopper remained in its current position, the greater the damage would be.

He gave me an absolute spray. I wasn't too fazed. I'd had a hell of a lot worse working for Milton Jones. He might have chewed me out for longer, but for the fact that the situation was quickly deteriorating. The spongy ground the skid was resting on was struggling to support the weight of the helicopter. It was slowly sinking before our eyes. There was no time to finger-point and level blame. We all had work to do.

The first task was to get the chopper upright. That meant getting into the water. We all got into extra-insulated dry suits and stepped in. The water was waist deep and bitterly cold. It felt like knives were being thrust into my legs. For the next 30 minutes, we took turns picking out 30-kilogram chunks of ice that had come loose when the chopper landed. Once all the ice was clear, we jacked up the tail boom and rolled a couple of large pieces of timber under the skids.

Progress was slow. The problem was the weight of the chopper. This is where the empty drum came into action. Using a hose, we sucked out three quarters of the fuel in the tanks. We also pulled out all non-essential items from inside the fuselage. If it wasn't fixed into the helicopter, it was taken out.

After a couple of hours, we had cleared enough ice under the chopper and taken enough weight out for Mike to attempt to lift it up. Using every inch of rope, I rigged the squirrel to the sling connected to Mike's chopper. He was flying the AS350.

The rigging drew out as Mike repositioned himself above the jet ranger. The ropes went taut as he very carefully started to lift the chopper out of the water. The Jet Ranger was too heavy for Mike to lift completely clear of the hole. We managed to slip a few pieces of large timber under the skids and stabilise the machine, but it remained partly submerged.

'That's great, Mike!' I shouted into the radio. I unhooked the sling and gave him the thumbs up. Mike flew off to collect the surveyors higher up the mountain.

I looked at the Jet Ranger. Water was lapping at the doors of the fuselage. It looked in a pretty sorry state. But I was confident that I would be able to fly her out.

'So who's coming up the front with me to help fly this thing out?' I asked.

Everyone laughed.

'You're on your own, Matt,' said Zonk.

I didn't blame them for being worried. When the blades start turning on a chopper, things can be thrown out of balance. It was easy to imagine the chopper slipping off the timber during the start up. There was also the possibility the chopper had suffered damage to the undercarriage or the tail boom when it fell through the ice. There was no way of knowing until Cory conducted a full inspection of the aircraft. But I needed at least one person up front with me. The chopper's resting position had pushed its centre of gravity towards the back of the machine. The more weight I had up front, the less likely the chopper would slip back.

'C'mon,' I pleaded. 'It'll be fine.'

'I'll do it,' said Cory. It took guts for him to volunteer. It was something that sealed our friendship.

'Thanks, mate,' I said.

We climbed into the Jet Ranger and I hopped into the pilot's seat. I'll admit, there were a few nervous moments as I cranked her up and the blades started turning. There was no warm-up. I went straight to full throttle. Our improvised pad was so unstable, I figured the less time we spent on it the better.

The chopper started to shudder. One of the timber logs was coming loose. I suppose I could have powered down. But this was our best chance. If I aborted now, the machine would most likely be stuck in this hole until the end of winter. It was now or never.

It took about a minute for the gauges to come up to 100 per cent. I lifted up the collective and we slowly rose. Even though I had dramatically reduced the weight of the machine, the chopper felt heavy. Something was wrong. I looked at the instrument panel. There were no warning lights coming up or any other indication of a problem. It wasn't until Zonk called me on the radio that I realised the problem.

'Hey Matty,' he said. 'You're towing a bit of a garden.'

There was no way of seeing the reeds from my position, but someone took a photo and showed me later. The Jet Ranger looked like Luke Skywalker's X-wing in that scene in *The Empire Strikes Back*, where Yoda lifts the spacecraft out of the bog in the Dagobah System. I kept the chopper in a low hover while the guys on the ground pulled off all the reeds. The improvement in the handling of the chopper was instantaneous. Once all the reeds were removed, I flew the chopper to a dry patch of land. Cory went over everything with a fine-tooth comb – the chopper was in perfect working order. More importantly, Zonk didn't fire me!

15

Croc Bait

In total, I spent four years in Canada. I would return to Australia towards the end of each year in preparation for the egg-collecting season. My first taste of collecting croc eggs at Moroak had left its mark. I was hooked. It became a yearly ritual that I continue to this day: a three-month adventure that bookends my year.

People often ask me why I keep doing it. It's a fair question. The risks involved are numerous and it isn't as if the money is all that great. Although I'm a firm believer in egg harvesting as a conservation measure, that isn't enough to draw me out year after year. It comes down to one simple fact. I love it.

I love the thrill of clearing a nest while being stalked by one of the world's greatest predators. I love the intense camaraderie with the boys, knocking back a beer and swapping stories at day's end. Most of all, I love the challenge and adventure of the job. Taking part in any activity that takes you to your limits – that demands every shred of experience and physical endurance to perform and survive – is living life to the max. For me, that's the only way to live.

* * *

The next couple of chapters recount some of my more memorable experiences collecting off crocodile nests. They are incidents that took place at some point in the 10 years I've been egg collecting and don't necessarily run chronologically. They provide a glimpse of the life of a collector and give an idea of how the industry has evolved over the last decade. I'll start with a technique of collecting eggs that is so dangerous it's no longer used. We called it the floating mat method.

Floating mat is a term collectors use to describe the native grass that grows at the edges of the big rivers and lakes of the Top End. The grass spreads out from the bank and across the water and provides the perfect conditions for crocs to hunt. The floating mat is thick enough to support the weight of an animal, but not so thick as to prevent a croc from bursting through and dragging unsuspecting prey to the murky bottom. For this reason, floating mat is one of the preferred places for crocs to build nests and one of the most dangerous places for humans to venture.

The nests are like little floating islands that are constantly patrolled from beneath. The moment an egg collector sets foot on floating mat, he or she is on a ticking time bomb. The crocodile feels the disturbance in the water and swims undetected beneath the mat. Stalking from below, the croc waits until the person stops moving. If the collector remains still for too long, he or she will be in the jaws of a crocodile before knowing what has happened.

Collecting eggs on floating mat is all about speed – get in and get out. That means landing the chopper as near as possible to the nest and reducing the amount of time the collector stands on the mat. Large inflatable floats would be fitted to the skids. The pilot would keep the rotor spinning so that the chopper would remain light on the skids to enable a quick getaway. It's easier said than done.

Landing a chopper near a nest or hovering over a nest is never a good idea. The moment a female croc is exposed to the intense vibration or noise from the chopper she becomes shaken and confused. Usually, she will be panicked into making uncalculated launches into the air, snapping at anything and everything. You are better off landing away from the nest and coming in slowly and quietly by foot to cause minimal disturbance. Although this is a preferable method, it is time-consuming, inefficient and risky in other ways.

Floating mat is by no means stable. At any minute, it might give way, leaving the collector waist-deep in water with a croc lurking and no easy avenue of escape. It also means a collector spends more time in the very place saltwater crocodiles like to hunt.

On one occasion, I was sitting at the controls of my R44 waiting for a couple of blokes to clear a nest. Even with my eyes glued to the water, there was no warning of a crocodile lurking beneath the floating mat. The first I knew that we were being hunted was when a big female burst through the grass with jaws open and tried to take a chunk out of the chopper. After failing to get any purchase on the underside of the chopper, she turned her attention to the cockpit, leaping up and knocking the window with her head.

Both of the blokes on the nest saw what was happening and dived for the chopper. They seemed to take an age to get completely inside. It took all my restraint not to pull up. A passenger is either in a chopper or out of a chopper, never half and half. If you take off with a person off balance while standing on the skids, that person will probably die.

'Hurry the fuck up!' I shouted.

Once everyone scampered aboard and strapped in, I pulled up. The croc had her head resting on one of the skids and was lifted off the ground for a second before falling back in the water. That was a close one. But not nearly as close as the day Bluey decided to bring his 16-year-old daughter Rainey on a day of collecting eggs on a floating mat out at the Moyle River near Coolibah. How nobody died that day is a miracle.

Located in the northwest corner of the territory, the Moyle cuts across seasonally inundated grassland. It's remote, swampy and full of crocs. Milton was flying with Bluey in one of the R44s. Meanwhile, I was flying Rainey in the R22. In placing his daughter in my chopper, Bluey was entrusting her safety to me. I hated every bit about that day. I'm all about fostering interest in wildlife among young people, but clearing nests on floating mat is no place for a 16-year-old.

Not that Rainey seemed bothered. She was having a blast, leaping around on the mat and carefully loading up her crate. I was sat at the controls keeping the chopper steady, with a pistol at my feet. By now I had cleared enough nests on floating mat to know that there was no way of accurately predicting where an attack would come. Having a gun nearby was a necessary precaution.

Rainey had done a good job. We had been going all morning and were approaching lunch. Rainey was filling up one last crate before we returned to the house to unload. The moment she strapped the crate in the chopper and leapt inside was a huge relief. Maybe we would get through this day without incident.

'Let's go back and get some lunch,' I said.

'Sounds good,' she said.

As we were getting airborne, Rainey pointed towards Bluey, who had just exited Milton's chopper and was about to clear another nest. Rainey was pulling out her camera and preparing to take a photo when a huge croc burst through the floating mat out of the water and grabbed her dad around the chest. The pain must have been incredible, but Bluey's face remained impassive. The split second it took for the croc to burst out of the water was like something out of a Hollywood movie. Rainey screamed.

You always know the danger is there but seeing it in action takes your breath away. I've had a lot of close calls with floats torn off and seats ripped out but seeing someone getting taken makes you realise how dangerous the work really is.

As Bluey was being taken towards the water, years of experience around crocodiles must have kicked in. He reached for his gun with his free hand while the croc tried to drag him into the water. Milton brought the chopper in a hover above Bluey, which scared the croc, who freed Bluey and took off. Bluey was unbelievably lucky he wasn't dragged into the water. All I could think was thank Christ it was Bluey and not his daughter. A slight girl like Rainey would not have stood a chance.

I remained nearby in a hover to see if they needed assistance. Bluey waved his arm to indicate he was okay and it was safe to land. Milton and I both landed quickly on some hard ground to inspect Bluey's wounds. Perfect teeth marks etched into his torso. He also had a couple of deep lacerations across his chest about an inch deep and some cuts in his back. He was understandably pretty shaken and we weren't medically qualified to know what the real damage was. Milton and I carried Bluey into the 44.

'Meet us at Palumpa,' Milton said.

A remote Aboriginal community, Palumpa has a small medical

facility and was about 15 minutes away. Rainey and I were dead quiet on the flight. From our perspective, it looked pretty bad. Surviving the initial attack didn't mean Bluey was out of danger. Crocodiles have a lot of power in their jaws and crushing down on a human torso could damage a lot of things.

On the way there I called the local clinic so the nurse could meet Milton's chopper on arrival. Milton pushed his chopper to the absolute limit, arriving a few minutes before us. After landing, Rainey and I raced into the clinic.

We pushed through the doors and to our astonishment, there was Bluey standing up with a bandage round his chest and a smile on his face. Rainey ran over and gave her dad a hug. Not many people end up in the jaws of a crocodile and live to tell the tale. Bluey is a hard old bastard, particularly when you consider he was back on a nest an hour later!

16

The Sling

It was clear the days of the floating mat method were numbered. We needed to come up with something new – something that improved safety, allowed the collectors to access the hard-to-reach nests and improved efficiency. Our solution was to start slinging collectors directly onto nests.

Long lining or slinging is a very efficient way to utilise a helicopter, whether it's fighting fires, logging or egg collecting. The slings I use consist of a high-tech polyethylene fibre capable of carrying up to 10 tonnes. This is massive overkill when your chopper can only carry around 350 kilos. Nevertheless, it gets the job done and keeps the fellas safe.

Slinging a collector onto a nest is all about reducing the time they are exposed to danger. In the early 1980s, when people began collecting crocodile eggs, they'd use a chopper to spot a nest and then land the collectors as close as possible. This was often kilometres away, requiring the collectors to walk into the swamps with only a rod and crate to keep them safe. It was very dangerous. They were exposed to heat exhaustion, deadly snakes and large male crocodiles patrolling the swamps.

Today, thanks to special conditions permitted to us from CASA, we're able to use the slinging technique with a double-hook set-up underneath the chopper. This means that the collector being slung underneath the chopper has a back-up hook if one breaks. We're the only people in the world sanctioned with these permissions and it makes our job a heck of a lot safer.

Using the slinging technique, we drop the collector into a nest where they unhook themselves and the chopper flies away. A collector must have all senses working to increase safety. If the helicopter remains hovering above the nest while the collector clears the nest, the engine drowns out the sound of approaching danger. Once the crate is filled, the collector will call the pilot back. The chopper returns, the collector reattaches to the sling and is winched off.

Being able to hop from nest to nest in this way is far more efficient, resulting in better daily yield of eggs. Plus, the collector conserves more energy, avoiding the long slog through cane grass and swamps. Approaching the nest from the air rather than by land also feels safer. From above, a collector often gets a visual of a crocodile and can better evaluate the risks of any given nest. If the guy on the sling feels the nest is too dangerous then he radios up to the pilot to move off.

But in terms of safety, the sling method is not foolproof. There are fairly obvious risks involved when you dangle a bloke from a 100-foot rope – otherwise known as a dope on a rope – and lower him onto a crocodile nest. For one thing, the weather becomes a real factor. The best sling pilot cannot predict a sudden gust of wind that might throw the collector into a tree or landing too hard on the nest. But the major downside of using a sling is exposure. Once the collector unclips from the harness, he is on his own. If he gets himself into trouble, only he can get himself out of it.

I don't look upon our early trials using the sling method on Milton's station with much fondness. They were cowboy days. At the time we didn't know any different – we were just trying to get the job done. Looking back, I can't believe the risks we took. Now, I wouldn't dream of operating how we did back then. Part of the problem was the lack of appropriate gear.

My good mate Jimmy and I routinely worked together. We were often slung under an R22. The 22 is a fantastic little machine – lightweight with great manoeuvrability and perfect for mustering. But with a load capacity barely above the weight of two adult males, it isn't suitable for slinging an egg collector lugging a full crate of eggs.

The chopper pilot would drop me onto a nest. While I was collecting, the chopper would pick up Jimmy and put him on a nest. I'd call the chopper back when I was done. And on it went. We'd work on rotation like this until all of the nests were cleared. We only had one harness. That meant one of us had to make do with a makeshift swing made out of a wooden plank. The unlucky bastard who scored the plank was always in for a hairy ride. There aren't too many experiences in life as terrifying as balancing on a piece of wood attached to a cable holding a full crate of eggs while a croc nips at your ankles.

But whether you were being slung on the plank or on the proper harness, the danger was ever present. I'll never forget the day I was on a nest packing eggs as Jimmy was being dropped on a nest not too far away. Over the radio I heard him start to bellow.

'Fuck me!' he screamed. 'Get me the fuck outta here!'

Jimmy had launched himself up in the air and started monkeying up the sling.

'Fuck that nest!' he shouted. 'Time for lunch.'

His face was pale when I saw him. Over lunch he told me he'd been lowered into a spot with two dead crocodiles and a few upturned turtle shells floating around. Just as he was being set down on the nest, he saw a head emerging from the murky waters the size of a 44-gallon drum.

That was one of Jimmy's close calls. We all have them. One constant element of collecting crocodile eggs is unpredictability. It doesn't matter how much experience and knowledge you've built up, the risk is always extreme. In my time, I've had three close calls while collecting eggs. Each of them was memorable for different reasons.

The first happened a few years ago. The team went out to clear a whole batch of nests along the Daly River. At this stage, I was working for the Professor. The Professor is Mick Burns, another legend of the Territory. We call him the Professor because he's one of the Darwin's most astute businessmen. The *Northern Territory News* recently named Mick the most powerful man in the NT. He has a broad set of business interests that include property development and ventures in the liquor industry. But it's the crocodile industry where he has really made his mark. He owns and operates one of the largest crocodile farms in the world. The 30-acre enclosure employs over 50 people and holds over 10 000 crocs.

Mick's a mentor and a mate, and a person I trust completely. Having trust in your teammates is absolutely vital when you're collecting. That's particularly the case when collecting along the

Daly River. For some reason the crocodiles out there are absolutely horrendous: the nastiest, crankiest and biggest bloody crocs in the country. Of the 30 nests we cleared on that day, Mick and I were attacked on 29 of them. Each croc seemed to be progressively more aggressive than the last.

It all came to a head at the end of the day. I was on the sling, being slowly lowered onto a nest completely hemmed in by cane grass. In the old days, these nests would be approached by land. Getting through the tall cane grass was a nightmare. There was no way through it other than by laying it down and moving over it. It was tough going and extremely dangerous. Being lowered in on a sling is a far better way to get to the nests.

I landed next to the nest. I had a stick in one hand and the crate in the other. I unhooked from the sling and gave the all clear to the chopper pilot. The chopper flew off and went scouting for another nest. The Professor, meanwhile, was slung in under another chopper to give me support.

Before I'd even set the crate down and inspected the eggs, this huge 13-foot female came thundering out of a tunnel she'd burrowed under the grass. I turned round to meet the attack with my stick. She was too quick for me. She got under the stick and knocked me back. I fell hard on my side against the cane grass. I was completely trapped. The croc lunged for me and I braced myself for the pain of being bitten. But nothing happened. The croc ended up resting her head next to my leg.

I looked skyward and immediately realised what was happening. The boom of the rotor wash coming from the hovering chopper had spooked the croc. I could hear the Professor instructing his pilot on the radio.

'Get me down lower!' he shouted. 'Hold here!'

The Professor drew his nine-millimetre semi-automatic and was taking aim. There are two reasons why I have never liked bringing guns onto nests. Firstly, we are not there to kill or harm crocodiles. We are there to harvest their eggs. Secondly, introducing firearms to unpredictable situations tends to increase the danger rather than reduce it. There are many examples of this fact.

In 2008, two of my mates Jase and Zac were dropped off on a floating mat. Trees were in the way so they were dropped a little distance from the nest. Zac stayed back near the chopper because the floating mat would not support the both of them. He stood guard with his pistol to cover Jase as he made his way to the nest. As he began opening the nest, the croc launched out of the water and grabbed him on the arm. Zac instinctively drew his weapon and fired a couple of shots at the croc's head to prevent Jase from being pulled under the mat. The animal was thrashing around so violently that the bullet missed its target. Instead, it hit Jase in the elbow. The croc let go and disappeared, unharmed. Jase on the other hand was left with his arm torn apart by a croc, his elbow shattered by the bullet. In the end, the bullet did more damage than the crocodile. He faced a long road to recovery.

This story was going through my mind as I looked up at the Professor wildly swaying back and forth on the sling, trying to take aim. For all his brilliance as a croc handler, the Professor is not known to be a crack shot with a gun.

'Wait! Don't shoot!' I shouted. 'I'll handle it.'

The Professor nodded, but kept the gun handy. I edged my leg backwards to give myself room and gave the croc a quick sharp kick to the head. It was a huge gamble – the sort of move that just as easily could stir her into attacking me. This time, I got lucky. The croc was startled and scurried off.

I don't want to downplay the seriousness of that moment. But even if that croc had grabbed hold of me, I stood a good chance of survival. The nest where I was attacked near Daly River was slightly unusual in that water wasn't lapping against it. She would have had to drag me at least 10 metres to get me into the water. Whether I would have kept all my limbs is another story.

That was the first time a crocodile nearly got me. The second time was even closer. It happened on the Tiwi Islands. The Tiwis are a group of 11 islands, including Bathurst and Melville, located about 80 kilometres north of Darwin. This is a hot, humid and wild place. Nine of the islands are uninhabited and the total human population on the remaining two comes to 3000.

With little human interference, the Tiwi Islands have incredible biodiversity. A whole lot of weird creatures thrive there, including masked finches, canary white-eyes, Tiwi masked owls, olive ridley turtles, Tiwi hooded robins, Carpentarian dunnarts, crested terns, and many more. There are also a huge number of saltwater crocodiles. They clog up the islands' coastal estuaries and rivers. Come the wet season, the Tiwis are fertile country to harvest croc eggs.

The Tiwis are usually one of the last stops of the egg-collecting season, as the land needs a lot of rainfall for the crocs to lay their eggs. I usually go out beforehand to spot nests before we collect them. I do this using an R22 and an iPad that gives GPS fixes on all the nests. Then using the data I've collected, the team and I plan the best approach to clear the nests, taking into consideration the gnarly rains and storms that hit that area. It's not uncommon for us to find ourselves collecting in a cyclone, which isn't very fun. One particular time, we were on our last day of our last run for the season. The team consisted of Mick Burbidge, Mick Jakobi, Craig Moore (also known as Wolverine on account of his beard), the Professor, Andy McLymont and myself. The two Micks were doing the flying.

Provided the weather is clear, the Tiwis are generally an easy enough place to collect because it's fairly dry and the crocs are small. The Professor and Wolverine were on a nest. Burbidge, meanwhile, was slinging me onto a nest close by. I unhooked and Burbidge flew off. I had a quick look around. It was dry shrubby country on one side with a waterhole on the other. Experience has taught me that a crocodile usually attacks from the water. So I set myself up accordingly.

I put the crate near the water, stick next to my leg and started to unfold the nest. It wasn't that big and neither were the eggs. I knew the female wasn't going be too much trouble. But the smaller the croc the more quick and cunning they are. For that reason, my hearing was strained and my eyes were intermittently scanning for slightest movements. I heard a couple of cracks come from the bush behind me. I paid no attention. I thought it was the shrubs rebounding after I stepped on them. I didn't even bother turning around.

Mosquitos were buzzing in my ears, driving me mad. Sweat poured down my face like melting ice on a hot day. It was the end of the season. I was tired, fatigued and ready to head home. I had marked about 10 eggs and placed them in the crate when I heard another crack, this time louder than before. I turned around and still saw nothing.

I moved back around to grab another egg from the nest, when the bush behind me came alive as a croc exploded at me with its mouth open. I had committed the cardinal sin of egg collecting.

I had made an assumption about where an attack might come from. When a collector makes assumptions, things tend to go wrong.

It all happened in slow motion. I fell backwards as the croc jumped up at me. I remember seeing her jaws wrap around my arm. I haven't got the first clue how that croc didn't take off my arm. I managed to grab the side of her head using my body weight to fling her away. But she came at me again straight away, pushing me closer to the water. I managed to kick the crate at her as I crawled back towards the water. I was hoping she would grab hold of the crate. No such luck. Turned out she had no interest in the crate. She was only interested in me.

The croc launched over the crate and came for me. I had just enough time to grab hold of the stick and wedge it into her mouth. Although not huge, the crocodile had tremendous power. She propelled backwards straight into the water. My concern wasn't the croc on top of me. I knew I could tire her quickly. I was more worried about her mate lurking in the water behind me.

Luckily, the water was only waist deep. I eventually got my footing. I pushed her to the side and she realised she'd been beaten. She took off through the water like an arrow, disappearing out of sight. I crawled onto the nest, radioed Burbidge and told him to come and get me. With that, the season was officially over.

17

The Ring

There had been a string of near misses and close calls. A feeling of doubt started to creep into the operation. If things didn't change, someone was going to get killed. The Professor challenged us to come up with safer methods of collecting croc eggs. We got together and came up with the idea of a ring.

The ring is a lightweight fence encased in a thick, brightly coloured plastic sheet similar to canvas, with metal ribbing on the inside. The material is similar to an air-conditioning duct but on a larger scale. It's about five feet high with a five-foot diameter – wide enough to fully enclose a nest – and attaches to the collector's harness. It serves as a visual barrier between the collector and any crocodiles patrolling the nest. At first, it was a resounding success. The crocs didn't know what to make of it. But just like every other invention devised to *improve* safety while collecting croc eggs, the ring doesn't *guarantee* safety. I learnt that for myself out at the Arafura Swamp.

The Arafura Swamp is a massive inland wetland in the middle of Arnhem Land. Prior to helicopters, large sections of the

swamp were totally inaccessible. Covering an area of 1300 kilometres at the peak of the wet season, the swamp is a jungle
paradise where everything grows big, from the giant barramundi
to massive spiders. But nothing comes bigger out here than the
crocs. The Arafura Swamp has the largest population of breeding
crocodiles in the world.

My mate Gecko was slinging me onto a nest in the middle of a
large area of black water. This was a nasty job. With black water
completely surrounding the nest, the attack could come from anywhere. Normally I'd have called up to Gecko and told him this
one was no good. But the ring had me overly confident. I gave
Gecko the all clear and down I went.

On landing I unclipped from the sling and unhooked myself
from the ring. The moment you unclip yourself from the sling,
your lifeline is gone. I did a full visual inspection and couldn't
see any croc activity. I extended the rod and checked the depth
around the nest. The nest was built up on an old tree stump.
From the edge of the nest, the water dropped straight down. The
water was deep too, certainly over eight feet. That was bad. If
a croc managed to pull me in, they would never find what was
left of me. The question then was simple – where was the croc?
Experience and instinct told me that she was lurking nearby.

'Keep on the radio,' I said. 'I'll call you back when I'm done.'

'No worries,' said Gecko.

Gecko took off while I knelt down and pulled off the reeds
and leaf matter the croc had raked over the eggs to keep them out
of the sun. I had a false sense of security in the ring and took my
time collecting on the nest. When I finally got to the eggs I discovered the nest was a dud. Most of the eggs were rotten and cracked.
This happens from time to time. This nest was probably flooded

and the eggs were rolled around too much or they became water-logged. I started collecting the eggs that were still intact, marking them before carefully placing them in the crate. Let me tell you a rotten nest enclosed in a ring is not a pleasant place to be.

I was all set to call Gecko back when something massive smashed into the side of the ring and knocked me on my arse. The croc had busted through the ring. Her snout was poking through and her teeth gripped onto the metal ribbing. I dug my feet into the ground and braced myself as she tried to pull the ring into the water. Even though I was unhooked from the ring, I was still trapped inside it. If the ring was going into that filthy black water then I was going in with it.

'Gecko!' I roared into the radio. 'Get your arse back here, now!'

I kicked the croc through the plastic meshing, hitting her right on the snout. She was a tough old girl. Even the full force of my boot didn't discourage her from getting the ring off the nest. Although these eggs would never hatch, a female doesn't aban-don the nest until the end of the wet season. At that point she will know the eggs are rotten. Until then, she will guard the nest with ferocious force.

With another heave, she managed to pull the ring further into the water. I estimated that a third of the ring was off the nest. I felt like I was on the edge of a precipice without a harness, liter-ally inches from certain death. I scrambled to my feet and grabbed hold of the rod, which had fallen to the ground. Reaching over the edge of the ring, I whacked that crocodile in the head three times. On the third hit, she released. I quickly manoeuvred the ring back into the centre of the nest while the croc backed off.

Looking down at her properly for the first time, my guess was that she was about 11 feet long. That's a good-sized croc. I've certainly encountered bigger in the wild, but never before had I been in a position of greater vulnerability.

The croc launched out of the water, brushing past my stick and snapping her jaws a few inches from my face. I had never seen a crocodile move that quickly before. Half her body landed on the railing, collapsing one side of the ring. I reeled back, falling hard onto my side, ending up about three feet from her jaws. I crawled back to the edge of the ring, doing my best to remain out of her strike zone.

'Gecko!' I shouted. 'Where the hell are you?'

'Nearly there.'

Not good enough, I felt like saying. The crocodile tried to attack again, but as she pushed off in my direction her back legs slipped on the edge of the nest. She slid a few feet back into the water. That little stroke of luck probably saved my life, allowing me enough time to get to my feet and push her back into the water with my rod. I danced around on that nest, keeping her at bay with my rod. Every chance I got I gave her a whack on the head.

By the time I heard the sound of the chopper I was nearly spent. Luckily, the croc was exhausted too. Her body was half on the nest and she was completely still. Gecko reckoned it took him two minutes to reach me from the moment I first called him back. It felt like two hours.

As the chopper lowered the sling, the rotor wash scared the croc away. She slid off the nest and vanished in the black water. I clipped what was left of the ring onto my harness and stole a quick glance skyward to see how Gecko was getting on. I was lucky to have him flying the chopper that day. On his first pass, he put that sling straight into my hand. I hooked on and bellowed at him to take me up. I catapulted into the air, the twisted ring dangling around my feet.

My hands shook all the way back to our pad. The pad is our base of operations, where the crates are loaded into the choppers. Even after I'd safely landed, it took me several minutes for the adrenaline to seep out of me. The boys had heard me swearing away on the radio but they didn't know the seriousness of it all until they saw me. I was ghostly white, my face and arms covered in mud.

'What happened to you?' asked Wolverine.

'Just a close one,' I said.

Everyone within earshot gave me a grim nod and went about his business. Don't think that the boys didn't care about my safety. All of us had forged a close bond. Working together in a job as specialised and as intensely dangerous as this one will do that. There's just no point bragging about it. Everyone has had a close call. It comes with the territory.

Showing off or big noting creates a macho culture, which is something we actively discourage. I'm not saying we're so hard and unfeeling that we don't have a yarn at the end of each day, laughing and shaking our heads in disbelief at some of the crazy shit that can happen on a nest. But we aren't cowboys with a point to prove. If someone tries to join our operation with that attitude they don't last long. The Professor will fire that person before he or she is killed. This is not a job for tough guys or show ponies. It's a job for professionals.

18

Flying on the Edge

I often get asked to describe the worst conditions I've flown through. It used to be a tough question to answer. After flying choppers for 15 years, you can imagine that I've seen some pretty shit weather. I used to tell people that in terms of the most challenging conditions, it was hard to separate flying in northern Canada and northern Australia. Both regions present different challenges.

During the Territory's wet season, the weather changes fast. One minute you will be staring at a clear blue sky, the next a column of black thunderheads will be barreling over the top of you, bringing lightning, howling wind and hail. The weather changes just as rapidly in the northern parts of Canada. Being caught out in a white out and having to fly on instruments surrounded by peaks and cliff faces is about as scary as flying gets.

But there was one day a couple of years back that tested me as a pilot like never before. It happened in the late summer, when the monsoonal rains and storms are most severe. Seven of us had been out collecting eggs for three days straight. We had been camping in an open field not far from Port Keats, a small coastal township roughly 400 kilometres southwest of Darwin. We knew there was a bit of weather about. On the day we left, a category one cyclone was coming into Darwin. Once it made landfall, the cyclone was expected to track southwest along the coast, right towards where we were collecting. We planned the trip so that we would remain one day ahead of the cyclone. The thing about cyclones is that they are unpredictable.

Things came to a head on the last day of the trip. I spent the day attempting to check the progress of the storm on my phone without success. The remoteness of our location meant there was limited service. That meant we had to run with instinct. There was no sign of tumultuous weather. It was a pleasant, cool day with a bit of drizzling rain. So we pressed on. Unbeknown to us, the cyclone had changed direction. It had turned west into the open sea, built into a category two cyclone and was now charging towards us. It was moving fast, too.

For six hours, we collected on the Moyle in perfect egg-collecting conditions, oblivious to the violence heading our way. We pressed further west towards the coast, eventually arriving at Table Hill, a small rise at the edge of the Indian Ocean. This was our final pit stop for collecting before we could head back to Coolibah Crocodile Farm to pass on the eggs. From here, we had a perfect vantage point to check the storm's progress. Far out to sea, spread across the horizon, was a line of black cloud. Things were about to get wild.

Here's the thing about collecting crocodile eggs. It's tough work. The people who do this job understand that you need to accept certain hardships. One of them is poor weather. If we cancelled a trip every time we ran into bad weather, no eggs would be harvested. Besides, if we pulled out now we'd have to return some other time. That was one headache we all wanted to avoid. So the boys suited up and got on with it.

One by one, the boys hooked onto a sling and I dropped them into the overgrown, croc-riddled jungle. The weather started to deteriorate quickly. The rain was coming in horizontal, spearing into the skin of each bloke on the sling like sharp needles. I had my head hanging out the window to check on the boys. The force of the wind and the rain was incredible. It felt like someone was working over my face with a pressure hose. But it was the sight of the boys on the sling being swung around like a wrecking ball that prompted me to call it off. The risks were now unacceptable.

I called the lads up on the radio and told them to hurry up and finish off their nests. The guys waiting back at the pad with the grounded choppers were happy to hear me over the radio. They had copped an absolute belting, too. I told them to have everything ready to get the hell out of there as quickly as possible.

I started pulling the remaining lads out of the jungle when Chris Wilson started howling on the radio to come grab him. Willow is a big, powerful lad with a cool head and laidback demeanor. If Willow is howling, something is seriously wrong.

I raced back to where I'd dropped him off, peering down through the rain. It took me a while to spot him. Even though I was hovering at an altitude of 100 feet, the rain was so heavy I could barely see the ground. Eventually, I caught sight of him. Willow was stuck halfway up to his waist in mud alongside a large croc nest. The swamp was filling up fast. In a few minutes, Willow would be underwater. But that wasn't the real danger. Lurking about three feet from where Willow stood was a large female crocodile.

Willow was frantically waving at me to lower the sling. I did my best to land the hook on top of him. I nearly had it in his hand, until a wind gust pushed it away. My heart was pumping through my chest, this was taking everything out of me and I couldn't imagine how Willow was coping down in the devil's lair. I took a deep breath and with every ounce of concentration I had, set my mind to the task at hand as the croc inched closer towards my mate.

On my second attempt, I put the sling right between Willow and the big female at the very moment she was lunging at Willow's head. The crocodile grabbed hold of the sling and immediately went into a death roll. As she wrapped herself up in the sling I saw an opportunity. I quickly pulled back on the collective and got her airborne for a few seconds, managing to drag her away from Willow. The croc untangled herself and landed in a pool of water scurrying away towards the ocean.

I whipped the sling back to Willow. He latched onto it like a magnet. I could hear him panting furiously through the radio. Once he was secure, I took him back to the staging area. Willow unclipped and I went back out to get the remaining blokes. Once I'd picked everyone up, I set the chopper down and gave the crew a quick rundown.

'I think this cyclone is on its way to us,' I said. 'It should still be out to the northwest so we'll be right to head northeast and southeast to get away.'

The plan was for Mick Jakobi and me to fly our choppers to Coolibah with the eggs. Meanwhile, Andy, our other chopper pilot, would take the boys back to Darwin. Everyone cracked on without hesitation. We loaded up the choppers with the crates and were airborne within minutes. Mick and I turned southeast, while Andy headed northeast. It was a relief to be leaving. At that stage, I was thinking the cyclone would make landfall at Table Hill. I couldn't have been more mistaken.

We were heading towards over the Fitzmaurice River. From there we would track up across to Bradshaw and end up in the valley of Coolibah Station. I calculated a flight time of about an hour and half. Aside from a few bumps, I was expecting a smooth flight. It very quickly became clear that we had misjudged the storm's location and direction.

The wind was picking up rather than dropping. Without warning, we were being hit with powerful updrafts followed by sudden downdrafts. It was unlike any turbulence I had experienced. The machine started rising and falling 100 feet at a time. The rain, meanwhile, was like a wall of water in front of us. The cyclone was actually south of our position and tracking northwards. We were on a collision course with it.

I was constantly on the throttle and collective to maintain rotor RPM. We slowed right up and made it over the first ridgeline into Madjilini Valley where the going was a little better. But we still had 100 kilometres of Kimberley country in front of us. I called into Mick.

'How you travelling?' I said.

'It's getting a little rough, bud,' he replied.

'Roger that,' I said. 'You stay in the valley. I'm finding it hard to see you. I'll stay high, you stay low.'

The wind became even more powerful as I climbed up the side of the escarpment. I could hear the machine moaning and groaning as I fed it more throttle to climb, doing my best to keep clear of the cliffs. As I reached the top of the escarpment a massive gust of wind smacked into me, causing the chopper to roll onto its side. I was squeezing the controls hard. My palms were sweaty and my knuckles white. It took every ounce of experience I possessed to keep that machine from spiralling out of control. My real worry was Mick, who had significantly fewer flying hours than me.

'Mick!' I called out again on the radio, 'How you travelling?'

'Getting smashed,' he shouted.

'Land if you get the chance,' I called back.

'I can't, mate,' he shouted. 'There's a wall of water coming down the valley in front of me and trees are getting airborne! It should be getting better soon though, right?'

I wished I could have said yes. I told him to hang in there. A couple of minutes later, Mick got back on the radio.

'It's getting a hell of a lot worse where I am,' Mick said.

'Tell me about it!' I yelled back.

A second later, I was hit by a downburst. The machine was pushed down into a ravine. The turbines roared as I gave her everything to make sure I didn't crash on the rocky bottom. Even though I was operating at full power, I couldn't get any lift. I had no choice but to go with it.

I dived into the ravine towards the river. It felt like I was in a kayak going down a raging river of rapids without a paddle. I made it into the valley and found some relatively stable air. I was now flying in the same airspace as Mick in poor visibility. I gave him a call to find out his whereabouts. Mick's sense of direction is questionable in even the most pristine conditions. For this reason, he was given the ironic nickname 'Homing Pigeon'. Other than being somewhere in the valley, Mick had no idea of his exact location.

'No worries, mate,' I said. 'I'll get back up top and try again.'

I managed to get some altitude, tracking alongside a spur. I was hoping to catch an updraft, but everything felt like it was pushing me back down. The wind was so strong the rain was coming into the chopper sideways. My machine was showing 100 knots on my airspeed indicator even though I felt like I was stationary. I looked down on the ridgeline below and the trees were being uprooted and folding over sideways like they were blades of grass. I kept thinking about the croc eggs, hoping they weren't getting too damaged from our rollercoaster ride.

Every little creek and watercourse below had turned into a raging river. Rocks, boulders and mud were sliding down the cliff faces. It was like the world was caving in. I maintained my course by using the ground as a visual. I was having a horrific time jumping from valley to valley across the top of the escarpment. Low cloud cover was becoming a problem too, whiting out the world and causing me to fly blind. I had to get this bird on the ground. I got back on the radio.

'I'm going try and find a clear spot on this escarpment to land,' I said.

'Roger,' Mick replied.

'What are you gonna do?'

Mick is a big-talker. Usually you cannot shut him up. On that day he was reduced to one- or two-word answers.

'Punching on,' he said.

Keeping that chopper in the air was taking up every ounce of his concentration. For both of us, this was flying on the edge.

I managed to get above the escarpment and found a small clearing hemmed in among a crop of big old gum trees. I took the chopper in slowly, ready at any minute to throttle up and pull out in case of an unexpected wind gust. I was only about 10 feet off the ground and looking good when a bolt of lightning forked down in front of me and struck a huge tree. The trunk disintegrated, sending splinters of wood flying everywhere. I pulled back from my planned landing and told Mick I was tracking further north to get out of the low cloud.

I kept pushing on, looking for a break in the weather. I knew it couldn't be too far off now. Mick and I kept in touch as much for comfort and encouragement as to ensure we didn't collide. Finally, Mother Nature calmed down. The sky opened up and I set a direct course to Coolibah Crocodile Farm. Mick called in to report that he'd made it through as well.

To say I was a relieved is an understatement. We were both lucky to get out. The weather had managed to separate us by 60 kilometres. It just shows how powerful those storms can be. When we finally landed at the croc farm we were met by an astonished Bluey. He couldn't believe we'd decided to fly through a cyclone. Had we known what we were flying into, we never would have done it.

When I fly back over the land now and see all the trees still strewn across the ground, it makes me appreciate the durability of the choppers we fly. I'm also reminded of just how important it is to keep a cool head and stay focused when the shit hits the fan.

19

Getting Down to Business

The nearly forgotten dream of starting a TV program came back to life during my first stint in Canada. The phone started ringing at three o'clock in the morning. I wasn't impressed. I had to be up in a couple of hours for work. I let it ring out. Whoever it was could wait. Then the phone started up again. I reached over and checked the call identification on the screen. It was an Australian number. I thought it was probably one of my mates back home ringing me pissed, so I let it go through to voicemail. The third time the phone rung I answered. I figured there could be an emergency.

'Hello,' I croaked.

'Matt,' said a chirpy voice at the end of the line. 'Nick Fordham here. I run a management company in Sydney.'

'Mate, it's three o'clock in the morning where I am. Can this wait until I'm a bit more human?'

'I want to talk to you about your show reels.'

That got my attention. Turned out Nick had heard about my early attempts to put a show together and was interested.

'I'm not home for a few months,' I said. 'Let's talk then.'

Nick was not the sort of guy to take no for an answer. He kept me on the phone for half an hour. He saw huge potential in the basic premise of a show but wanted to share a few ideas to make it bigger.

'If we can execute it in the right way, this thing will have global appeal.'

'Sounds good, Nick,' I said. 'Let's keep in touch.'

I'll admit to having more than a few doubts. Those three years I spent toiling away in front of and behind the camera had amounted to basically nothing. I later discovered that when it comes to television, most ideas never see the light of day. Hard work is not in itself enough to ensure success in television. A lot of it boils down to good timing and a bit of luck.

Nick was incredibly persistent. He rang me up on a weekly basis, setting down ideas, laying out plans and offering to represent me. It was hard to fault his dedication. He certainly managed to rekindle my enthusiasm for a show. But I was never going to go into business with someone I had never met. I needed to put him through his paces, see just how keen he was to get this show up and running. I had just the thing in mind.

Egg-collecting season was on the horizon again and I was heading back to Australia soon. I thought there would be no better way to start our partnership and show Nick what I'm about than collecting crocodile eggs together.

'Clear your calendar in late December,' I said to Nick. 'We're going egg collecting.'

Nick came up to Darwin a couple of days after Christmas. He had suggested we get some footage to show the networks. I got my mate Mark Priest to come along too. Mark is a top cameraman and good bloke. His passion is underwater filming and he has shot world-class footage of great white sharks that was picked up by Discovery Channel. He was exactly the right bloke for the job.

With two choppers, we all headed out to the Arafura Swamp. If ever there was a way of working out whether Nick was fair dinkum, it was sticking him on a nest in Arafura. Nick also thought he'd try his hand at a bit of camera work and borrowed a camera from his brother Ben, who worked at Channel 9.

Both Nick and Mark filmed from the choppers while Gecko slung me onto a few nests. We cleared a couple of nests without any problems. Then it was Nick's turn. I trained him up on how to clip on and clip off from the sling. This proved to be a real struggle for a city slicker like Nick. We were in fits of laughter as he fumbled his way through the equipment.

After a good old laugh, we got busy. We cleared a couple of nests together. They were easy ones – little water and basically nowhere for a croc to mount an ambush. To ensure nothing went wrong, I went in first to secure the nest. I'd then radio up and give Nick the all clear. Once he'd gotten the hang of it, we went looking for cracking nests with some cranky females to get some proper footage. This is where the real fun started.

The idea was to use Nick as a decoy. Once I had been dropped in close to the nest, Gecko slung Nick over and dangled his feet right above a crocodile. The sight of a man hovering above caused the croc to launch seven feet out of the water. Nick gave a new meaning to screaming for dear life. The poor bloke was packing it. I wished to God I had a camera to film the entertainment. While Nick was distracting the croc, I was able to approach the nest freely with a screen door. Once I was in position, Gecko dropped Nick in behind me. But if Nick thought his misery was over he had another thing coming.

Nick was lowered into waist-deep water full of leeches, snakes and spiders. As I went to unhook him from the sling, Nick begged me to leave him attached.

'Listen to me,' he said. 'I can get the shots from the air.'

There wasn't a chance in hell I was letting him off. I unhooked him and there we were together ready to advance on the croc nest. Nick was certainly as green as they come, but I've got to hand it to him – not too many people will volunteer to be slung around on a helicopter, much less being slung directly onto a nest with no experience of crocs in the wild. This guy was definitely serious about doing business with me.

As we approached the nest, I let a couple of gunshots go into the water to scare off the croc that was patrolling nearby. I gave no prior warning to Nick, who shat himself the moment I fired. As I was getting onto the nest, the croc scampered onto it at full pace and smashed into the screen door. After a couple of goes at the screen, the croc slunk back into the water. Nick quickly clambered up onto the nest, wisely keeping away from the edge of the water. I collected the eggs and we moved onto the next one. Nick wasn't pleased to hear there were more.

While all this was going on, Nick was doing his best to film me on his handy cam. When it comes to camerawork, let's just say Nick shouldn't quit his day job. In fairness, he was understandably preoccupied with not being eaten. Besides, this wasn't a test of his ability to film me in action. I wanted to see how he coped under serious pressure. For that reason, I saved the worst until last.

I spotted a horror nest propped up on an overturned log in

the middle of a swamp of more waist-deep water. There was one big girl sitting on the nest.

'This one looks good to me,' I shouted over the radio. 'Put us down here, Gecko.'

I had my crate, an eight-foot rod, a five-foot screen door and my pistol ready to go. As the chopper got closer, the rotor wash stirred up the croc and she began jumping at the chopper. At this point, Gecko flew over the nest providing Nick with his first look.

'No, no, no!' he shouted. 'We're not going in there.'

'Yes, we are,' I said.

On cue, the crocodile swam directly under me and started leaping out of the water. It was trying to pull me off the sling. Gecko saw what was happening and pulled up.

'You sure you want to go in?' he asked.

'You bet,' I said. We hovered for a while, waiting for the croc to move off. Eventually she backed down into the water, giving me a small window to drop down.

'Take me down!' I shouted.

Gecko put me on the nest. I landed in the water about 10 feet from the nest. I unclipped from the sling and Gecko took off. Nick came in next, right behind me. He was beside himself, even more than before.

'This is fucking ridiculous!' he shouted.

'Start filming!' I shouted back.

'What the fuck is that?' Nick shouted, pointing over my shoulder.

On the other side of the nest, the croc was charging towards us. She was swimming fast enough for a wake of white water to trail off her head. I lifted the screen door, drew my pistol and pulled the trigger. I fired three times, the bullets disappearing into the water directly in front of the croc. It made no difference. She kept coming.

'Bring the chopper back!' Nick shouted.

'Calm the fuck down and get over here!' I shouted.

Nick shimmied in behind me and started filming as the croc barrelled into the screen. She hit me with such force the screen was knocked out of my hand. That was a pivotal moment. I was knocked off balance and exposed. Had the croc launched an immediate second strike, I would have been gone. Luckily, she circled back around to build up a head of steam for another attack. I took hold of the shield and held it in front of me as she charged in towards me again and again.

Sensing the fight was draining out of her, I holstered my pistol and started pushing her away with my stick. I managed to clear a path to the nest.

'Stay close,' I said to Nick. 'She'll come again.' There was no need to ask Nick to stay close. He was stuck to me like a Siamese twin. Nick muttered something under his breath. I stole a quick glance behind me and had to suppress a smile. His eyes were as big as saucers and his face was ghostly white. I don't blame him for shitting himself. Approaching a nest in the water is about as dangerous as this job gets.

We waded through the water. A few feet from the nest, Nick scurried up onto the dry ground. He was breathing heavily, scanning the water for telltale signs of crocodile activity. I knew it was only a matter of time before that big female would recharge her batteries and have another crack. I got on the radio and called the Wolverine in for back-up. The Professor and the Wolverine are the only two fellas that I'd ever call in to deal with a croc like this one. Craig got lowered in and at the same time I heard

Gecko's voice crackle over the radio.

'There's another nest about 100 metres north of your position,' he said.

I turned round to Nick.

'Ready to go one more time?' I asked.

His face dropped. But he nodded his consent. We ended up working until day's end. There was a lot of action that day. We were all looking forward to seeing what Nick had shot. But when we looked back at his footage it was like we were watching a reel from *The Blair Witch Project* – lots of erratic footage, heavy breathing and absurd noises. It certainly wasn't quality viewing. It's a good thing we had the footage Mark had captured from the air.

'I'll take this back to Sydney and rustle up some interest,' Nick said. 'I promise you I'll make it work.'

I needed no further convincing. It's one thing to talk a big game, it's another to come out and clear nests. Nick had put his faith in me. The least I could do was return the favour.

Nick was good to his word. He knocked on a lot of doors, worked the phone hard and persisted in the face of constant rejection. Nothing much happened for the first two or three years, just a whole lot of empty promises. Nick warned me that this might happen. Show business is a fickle game. We just needed to hang in there. Eventually, Nick said, we would catch a lucky break.

He was right.

20

Monster Croc

I'd been called onto a job up at La Belle Station, a huge property next to Litchfield National Park in the northwest corner of the Territory. The station owner wanted a number of crocs that were tearing through the station's livestock removed. I was starting to make a bit of a name for myself as a croc catcher. With the crocodile population increasing, I was getting called more often. I was happy to help out. The Professor's croc park in Darwin needed more crocs for breeding and I enjoyed the work. It was the perfect way to mix things up between mustering and heli-fishing work.

This was a hell of a big job. The work was relentless. I had to base myself out at the station for over a month, croc catching day and night. My main aim was to catch mature females around the nine- to 12-foot mark, along with a few adolescent males that were sometimes over 14 feet. I also got the tip-off about a few larger crocs that needed to be taken out.

Catching large crocodiles is an exhilarating, difficult and time-consuming activity. The process begins with a thorough investigation of the crocodile's habitat. You have to think defensively, looking for signs and track marks in wallows indicating a croc's place of rest. It's important to critically survey the land and identify the spots where you think the crocodiles stalk their prey. It's in these spots where you set your traps.

After the areas of interest have been scouted and the hot spots identified, a plan is put in place to lure the crocodile into a trap. For the bigger crocs, it isn't possible to simply stick a dead pig in a cage and wait for the crocodile to be caught. Something more imaginative is required. Equipment, fencing, supplies and boats all need to be slung out to the location. After a portable fence is constructed around the area of interest, an intricate set-up of ropes and pulleys is hooked up to a trapdoor.

Clayton Howse and Paul 'Benny' Benbow – old school mates of mine from South Australia – flew up to help me catch some of the smaller crocs. Clayton and Benny were right into their surfing and loved an adventure. Most of the time their escapades consisted of big waves, jetskis and the ocean. This was their first taste of choppers, pigs and swamps. The boys helped me build contraptions, sling traps and shoot pigs for bait during the day. At night we were out on the water catching crocs from the boat. They were having a cracking time.

One night, Garth – the station owner's son – told us a story about an elusive crocodile that made his way around a waterhole on the station. People had only ever caught glimpses of the big male. There were no photographs, just stories of 700-kilo bullocks found on the banks of the waterhole, literally snapped in half. The croc had become the stuff of legend, the Top End's version of the Loch Ness monster. Some people doubted its existence. But Garth and his family knew he was real. Garth had wanted to catch the monster croc, but his old man told him to steer clear.

A croc that size was too dangerous to catch.

Garth's story got my heart pumping. He told me the where-abouts of the waterhole. That was where I would set the trap. At first light the next morning, Clayton, Benny and I slung the boat over to the waterhole and got to work. Before we built the trap, I wanted to properly scope out the area. We worked into the night, catching smaller crocs swimming in the waterhole and tying them off at the side of the bank. The boat was a 12-foot-long tinny. The small size meant we were forced to return frequently to the bank to unload our catch.

Around midnight, having just tied off a couple of five- and six-foot crocs on the bank, Clayton's spotlight lit up what we thought were a set of golden crocodile eyes on the far side of the waterhole. Off we went to investigate. Clayton kept the torch trained on those eyes the whole way across. As we came closer, he played the light along what we thought was the crocodile's body. Instead, Clayton lit up a massive, black log with two perfectly etched holes at the base of its trunk that from a distance looked like eyes.

Without warning, the engine started to cough and made strange crunching noises. We had taken the tinny into shallow water. The propeller was becoming entangled in weed. I killed the engine. I'd have to reach into the water and untangle the prop. I told Clayton to keep a look out with the spotlight while Benny came back to help me out.

It was a moonless, pitch-black night. Every so often, forks of lightening would touch down on the horizon. Seconds would pass before a low rumble of thunder would roll across the water hole, scaring off the native birds nesting on the banks. Clayton contin-ued scanning the water around the boat, then he froze. We all felt it.

The energy in the air seemed to shift. We were in the presence of something big.

'Fellas,' I said, calmly as possible. 'Stay back from the side of the boat and keep a keen eye out.'

We all had our eyes scanning the area around the boat when there was a sudden explosion of water. Clayton swung the torch around to where we heard the splashing and lit up what we had mistaken for the massive log.

'Lads, that log is moving towards us,' Clayton said.

'Holy shit,' I said.

My brain was struggling to register what I was seeing. The massive log was a massive crocodile. It's difficult to judge the length of a crocodile when it's half submerged in water in the dead of night. But I could say with absolute certainty that this was one of the largest crocodiles I had ever seen, and I've seen a lot of them. We had just stumbled onto the monster croc Garth had told us about the previous night. More concerning was the fact the tinny had drifted between the crocodile and its path to deeper water. With the propeller still tangled up in weed, we were dead in the water.

Benny was the first to pipe up.

'Come on, fellas,' he said. 'Let's have a crack and catch it. This might be our only chance!'

As much as I admired Benny's attitude, I don't think he realised the enormous size of this animal. Clayton kept the light on the croc as he came towards us. I whispered to the boys not to move or make a sound as he approached the boat. The croc came straight to the front of the tinny then down the right-hand side, pushing us to the bank like we were just another piece of leafy debris. I kid you not: his head looked like it was half the side of the boat. You could hear every scale scraping down the side of the tinny.

The lads were completely psyched. They were revelling in the experience of seeing such a massive animal up close and personal. I was less enthusiastic. We were in serious danger. An animal this large could flip the tinny over with a swipe of his tail. It was highly unlikely we would survive a midnight swim back to the other side of the bank.

His head passed alongside the tinny. Nervous as I was, the sheer length of the animal was awe-inspiring. He slowly worked his way towards the back of the tinny and then cruised off into the night. I breathed a massive sigh of relief. I told Clayton and Benny to keep their eyes peeled while I finished untangling the prop. Once I'd removed all the weeds, I fired up the engine and we returned to the bank.

I was buzzing the next morning. I wanted to get everything in place to catch this croc. But I needed more experience on the team, someone who knew how to handle big crocodiles. I got on the phone to the Wolverine. He didn't take much convincing. After I told him what I had seen the previous night, he was practically out the door before hanging up the phone. I spoke to La Belle's station owner Peter Camm too, and told him I needed more help. He gave me Garth and his daughter Amelia. Garth had his chopper licence, which was very handy, and Amelia proved a massive help too.

Now it was time to set up the trap. I returned to the homestead and started slinging the gear out to the water hole. We picked a place on the south side of the waterhole, right where we had seen the croc the night before. Then came the hard part.

Crocs do their hunting from the water. Therefore, in order

to lure crocodiles into the trap, the panels need to be built into the water. Someone has to get into the croc-infested waterhole to fix the panels and the door. Being exposed in waist-deep murky water is the most dangerous part of the operation. It's impossible to set up a trap without making a racket and drawing the attention of whatever lurks in the waterhole.

After a lot of hard yakka, we finally finished the trap. It was big enough to comfortably fit about 10 head of cattle. Now it was time to bait it. This was the part that Benny and Clayton loved the most. We jumped in the chopper and flew across the floodplain to get a few pigs. Soon enough we found a mob of about 20 or so. I dropped the boys out and told them that we needed four of the biggest pigs they could find. I flew away and rounded them up, pushing the mob of feral pigs towards the boys. For a couple of blokes like Benny and Clayton, a licence to hunt feral animals got their adrenaline pumping. I could see their smiles from the air.

They got what we needed without hassle. I'm not sure who shot what. One thing's for sure: they wouldn't stop arguing about who was the best shot and who shot the biggest pig!

We got back to the trap and hooked up our dead pigs to the side of the fence. We made sure half of the carcasses were submerged, bloodying up the water. While the other halves were left out to rot on the side of the fencing, stinking the place up something terrible. The dead pigs were tied to a rope hooked up to a trigger device on the trapdoor. When the carcass was pulled off the side of the fence, the door would slam shut, trapping the crocodile in the pen.

We got back in the chopper and let nature take its course. On the flight back to the camp, the sound of the helicopter sent hundreds of crocodiles of all sizes scurrying in the fright. This place was absolutely infested with them. I remember thinking at that point that this would be a good place to shoot a little piece about catching crocs. I didn't realise how quickly that passing thought would turn into a reality.

Next morning, I set out for the trap. On approach, I could immediately tell something had happened. The trap door was down and the water was stirred up around it. It looked like there was a croc caught in one of the wings, which had me puzzled. I landed nearby and jumped into the boat to go and investigate. As I pulled up to the trap there was a lot of thrashing going on and I could see a 14-foot croc with its head caught in the rails. I tried to get him out when I realised there was a second croc caught in the same panel, but this one was stuck under the murky water. I had to move fast to get this one out otherwise it would drown.

I started getting a rope around the one on the bottom of the rail when the water underneath the tinny just erupted. I grabbed hold of the top rail and pulled myself away from the crocs to see what was going on. There were tails, teeth and limbs coming out of the water left, right and center. A couple of panels on the trap looked like they were about to break free.

Then it happened – one of the most epic things I have ever seen in the wild. The monster croc we had been trying to catch roared out of the water with one of the other crocs in his jaws. He dragged him out past my tinny and tore him apart in the middle of the lagoon. The sheer power of the animal made me freeze. It took me a few seconds to regain my senses. I had to get moving. I managed to free the other croc caught in the panel, reset the trap and get the hell out of there.

The monster croc didn't return to the trap. I continued on the day-to-day work of clearing out the other crocs for the remainder of my time there. Benny and Clayton went home with some great stories to tell and Garth, Amelia and a young fella Ross gave me a hand to keep catching. Every day I went about catching crocs on La Belle, I kept my eyes open for that massive animal. Eventually, I came across him again.

It happened during one of my routine checks of the small traps. I saw him from my chopper, lying under a tree on the opposite side to where the trap was set. I hovered down in the chopper in front of him. We were eyeing each other off from about 10 feet apart. It was a highly charged moment. He was not in the slightest bit worried about me. The area looked like the perfect place to set another trap. All I had to do was get it around the tree he was laying under.

I landed back in a nearby paper bark swamp and walked up to his den. It was a great spot. He'd made a channel from the main lagoon and a deep wallow around the tree where he was laying in anticipation to ambush the cattle passing by. This is where I was going to catch the big fella.

The moment I got airborne, I was on the phone to Nick.

'I've just seen the biggest croc of my life,' I said. 'We should do a story on this and everything else that I've been doing over the last month.'

The timing could not have been better. Channel 7 had just launched its news magazine program, *Sunday Night*. It was modelled on *60 Minutes*, with a commitment to in-depth coverage of a story. Nick weaved his magic and got us on the third episode. He sold it to them as a something that was right up *Sunday Night*'s alley. The newsworthiness of the story was obvious. One of the largest saltwater crocodiles in Australia was ripping through cattle, horses and livestock on a famous northern cattle station.

It was also a story that cast a light on the broader issue of how to deal with excessive numbers of saltwater crocodiles threatening remote communities in the Top End since the ban on croc hunting.

Channel 7 loved the idea. Within a week, Samantha Armytage was on her way up to La Belle. Sam absolutely nailed the story. The 13-minute piece perfectly captured the savage beauty of the Territory, whilst providing a glimpse of life in the Top End. And, boy, did the crocs come out to play.

The camera crew got some great footage of me throwing a rope around the snout of a couple of gnarly fellas in a muddy bog and lifting them onto the back of a ute. The cinematography was stunning and perfectly portrayed the powerful beauty of these creatures. I also managed to trap a huge, 16-foot croc that we airlifted in a cage. The whole thing was capped off with a tense sequence shot at night in a tinny. We managed to rope a big boy into our boat. As we were preparing to haul him over the gunwales, Sam started crying. Her tears were completely valid, given the terror of the moment. It was the perfect storm for telly, although not much fun for Sam.

The story was as much a profile piece on me as anything else. The producer played me up as a kind of modern cowboy and homed in on the fact that I was single. On camera, I told the producer what I felt at the time about relationships: that they slow you down. I was totally committed to the work and had conservation goals and dreams. That for me was what it was all about.

I couldn't have been happier with how the whole thing went. There was only one problem. The massive croc never showed up. Some of the boys thought that we had actually caught the croc and that the size of the fella that ripped apart that 14-footer was not as big as we had imagined. But my instincts told me that he was still out there. Before Sam and the Channel 7 crew left, I moved the trap and reset it around the tree he had been lying under. When we returned the next day, a croc had taken the pig but didn't set off the trap. I leapt into the pen and inspected the huge prints left in the mud. They were clearly made by an abnormally large crocodile. I suggested to the producer that they stick around for a couple more days. He told me he had run out of time. Besides, they already had more than enough. It was frustrating. But there was nothing that could be done.

Channel 7 pumped a lot of publicity in the lead-up to the show. The episode enjoyed a ratings bonanza, providing a welcome boost to the general profile of the show. I took a call from Nick shortly after the episode aired. Channel 7 was stoked. The producer had contacted him to say that if I managed to catch the big croc, they would be prepared to air a follow-up episode, provided that they didn't have to foot the bill to shoot it.

By that time, I was catching crocs on nearby Welltree Station. I still had the trap in place at the old spot and was quietly confident that, provided there was bait in the trap, I would catch him. While working at Welltree, I regularly flew over the trap to throw a pig in. I left the trap unset so the crocs could come and go as they pleased. The best thing was that the big croc was also going in there and getting comfortable with the trap.

I set a few days aside and got on the phone to Mark Priest who flew up to help film me the action. The moment Mark was on the plane heading north, I hunted the biggest pig I could find. Once I'd bagged a big old boar, I rebaited and set the trap. As I was making noise and setting up the trap, I could see the big croc lurking outside the gate, watching my every move. I made sure

I did everything with razor-sharp precision. Once I was satisfied the panels were secure and the trigger mechanism on the door was working, I flew back to Darwin to collect Mark.

I didn't sleep a wink that night. I had a feeling the big fella was already in the trap. I wanted to get out there and have a look. It took an eternity for the sun to come up. At the first hint of light on the horizon, we were off flying out to the lagoon. I was bursting with excitement.

I kept high as I approached the nest. I didn't want to get too close in case I spooked him and he smashed apart the trap. I could see that something had stirred up the water inside the trap. I could also see a big tail sticking out. There was definitely a crocodile inside the trap. But the question remained – did we have the right one?

I landed the chopper and we made our way to the trap. As we approached, the big croc went nuts. It was definitely the croc we were after. He looked more like a dinosaur. He took a lunge for the panels and managed to get his front legs over the top rail, which was about six feet high. One more kick and he was over and out. Without thinking, I took off towards him and got underneath his chest. I pushed him up and to the side, making sure my head and arms where out of the reach of his jaws. He slid sideways and down the panels. He gathered up his energy and had a go at the gate. He rammed the gate with such force, that it bent the whole trap out of shape. I raced back to the chopper to get a few more panels and ropes to reinforce the trap. I wasn't letting him get away this time.

I made a few phone calls to get trucks, vehicles, ropes and manpower. Nick Robertson, a very experienced croc catcher based in Darwin, came out to sedate him. Nick and I managed to get a rope around his snout without too much trouble. After gaffer-taping his mouth shut and covering his eyes with a blind-fold, four of us pulled him out of the pen. We got him to the edge of the riverbank. The tricky part now was getting him across the river. There was no way we would be able to lift him onto the tinny. Weighing in close to a tonne, the animal's weight would probably capsize the boat. So I came up with a solution.

I tied the rope that was around his snout to the cargo hook of one of the choppers. With the help of the chopper, we man-aged to lay the front third of his body over the stern of the boat. With the back two thirds of his body dragging behind the tinny, we got him across the river to the tilt-tray truck waiting on the other side. From there, we took him back to the Crocodile Park in Darwin. We got out the measuring tape. His length was 18 feet, three inches. This was my biggest croc yet and one of the biggest ever captured.

Mark and I edited up the footage and sent it to Channel 7. Two weeks later I was on a plane to Sydney. We did a live show in front of a studio audience. I was sat on a couch fielding ques-tions from hosts Chris Bath and Mike Munro. We started off with a series of clips of me gaffer-taping the snout of the croc before airlifting the croc's head onto the back of the tinny. Then a producer came out with a measuring tape to indicate the incred-ible size of the animal.

After a commercial break, Sam Armytage joined us on the couch and discussed her experience reporting on me up at La Belle. The context provided by Sam, coupled with my foot-age and our live audience discussion told a good story. But then came the questions about girlfriends. It was becoming clear that my relationship status was going to come under scrutiny, which was uncomfortable for me. At that time I was 12 months into my first serious relationship and was trying to make a go of it, but the media attention didn't make it easy. The advice from PR people was that it didn't hurt being single. In fact, in all of my interactions with media to this day the question of whether I'm a bachelor or not is always a point of discussion. I was with my girlfriend Gemma for about four years; she is a beautiful, kind-hearted woman who supported me through a lot. Unfortunately, with the pressures of the media and work commitments, our relationship deteriorated and things came to an end between us. I find the attention on my relationship status very embarrassing and bizarre. Anyway, it's something I take with a pinch of salt and have a laugh about nowadays.

Another point raised during the *Sunday Night* show was around people drawing comparisons between me and Steve Irwin. Steve's conservation work is second to none. There are so many people who continue to be inspired by Steve, myself included. There are a few people who have done more for conservation in this country than Steve. I have nothing but respect for him. To be mentioned in the same sentence as him is a huge compliment. After all, Steve's life was dedicated to the same goal I am driving towards – raising awareness about animals in the wild and the dangers they face in the modern world. But I certainly don't aspire to be the next Steve Irwin. In my view, comparing me to Steve detracts from his legacy. So when I was asked whether I saw myself as the next Steve Irwin, I answered, 'Irwin was one of a kind. He did remarkable things for the country and for conservation.'

Following on from this, Chris Bath asked about the other areas I work in aside from crocodiles. It was an opportunity to spell out the sort of show that Nick and I were interested in creating. Yes, it was going to involve crocodiles. You can't do a show set in the Top End that doesn't include crocs. But there was also going to be stories covering the plight of wild brumbies, bull catching on cattle stations and the life of mustering pilots.

I couldn't have been happier with how everything went. It seemed to hit the mark. Sure enough, the next day, Nick's phone started ringing. Discovery Channel and National Geographic were lining up to make a show with us. Nick and I talked things over and decided to go with Discovery. It was an exciting time. This was the culmination of five years' work. The dream was about to become a reality. I was about to learn a hard lesson about how television works.

***

It all seemed so good at the start. A producer from Discovery touched down in Darwin, absolutely bursting with enthusiasm. She was genuinely excited about filming in the Territory and the potential of the new show.

'This is going to be huge!' she said in her strong American accent.

Her vision for the show was all about crocs. That was to be expected. The footage of me pulling the 18-foot monster out of the pen at La Belle had gone viral on the internet. This was what the audiences wanted. I told her that I hoped the show would be more than just catching crocodiles. She assured me that it would. But there is, she explained, a global fascination with these animals. The primary focus of the show initially had to be on crocs.

'We want to see you pull a croc out of a swamp,' she said.

'Okay,' I said. 'I can ring around and find out if there are any crocs that have been humbugging station owners.'

'I was hoping we could go to this place,' she said.

She handed me an online news article. The moment I saw the headline, alarm bells started ringing. It read, 'Croc kills Briony Goodsell in Black Jungle Swamp, Northern Territory'.

Briony was an 11-year-old taken by a croc at Lambells Lagoon near Black Jungle, about an hour's drive east of Darwin. Given the lagoon's distance from the coast, it was generally regarded as a safe place to swim and was a popular spot for locals. Briony got permission from her mum to take her younger sister down for a splash about in a swollen creek. Her mum had no reason not to let her go. Briony was a sensible girl who had swum in that creek hundreds of times before. Before she left, Briony's mum told her daughter to keep in the shallows.

The eldest of three kids, Briony jumped in. Her sister, Bethany, witnessed her resurface with a distressed look on her face. A friend heard her call out for help before she disappeared. She was never seen alive again. Other witnesses said that they saw a crocodile's tail slap the surface just after Briony went under. The cops called off the search later that day when Briony's remains were found washed up 450 metres downstream from where the attack took place. The coroner concluded that a 14-foot saltwater crocodile killed Briony. But the animal was never found.

'I want you to catch this croc,' she said.

'Not interested,' I said, without hesitation.

It was a slightly tense moment. The producer reminded me that she had creative control of the show. I didn't care. Under no circumstances was I going to profit from a family's tragedy.

'But isn't this a big reason why you capture crocs?' she asked. 'To protect the local community?'

I couldn't argue with her point. The producer then told me she wanted me to interview Briony's mother, Charlene. She believed that it was the most powerful way of drawing attention to the dangers that crocodiles posed to people that lived in the Territory. I agreed on two conditions. Firstly, Charlene had to agree to the interview. Secondly, I had the final say as to how the show was put together. The producer agreed. In light of her earlier wishes of creative control, I was pleasantly surprised.

I rang Charlene. It was one of the toughest calls I've ever made. It turned out that Charlene was more than happy to be interviewed. She was in the middle of a croc-management campaign to kill or remove all crocodiles within a 50-kilometre radius of Darwin. This would be a welcome opportunity to raise awareness.

We drove out to Charlene's place the next day to conduct the interview. The producer was fantastic during the interview. She was very in tune and sensitive, adding words of support during the interview. Charlene was incredible. She had a lot of dignity in the face of her tragedy. I didn't ask tough questions, I just let Charlene speak. After about an hour, we wrapped things up and were happy with how the interview went.

Now it was time to catch a croc. There was no point returning to Black Jungle. The police had trawled the area and turned up nothing. The crocodile would be long gone. I told the producer that we could be out there for months and never find a crocodile so we headed back to La Belle to pull out another big croc. I brought along Jimmy, my old mate from my days out at Moroak. Jimmy had as much crocodile experience as anyone. He was someone I had worked with for years and trusted with my life. He also brought a bit of character to the production.

Jimmy and I pulled out a 14-footer from a creek. It wasn't as big as the croc that we caught for *Sunday Night*. But it was feisty. We roped a few crocs in a bog and pulled them onto a ute. It all came up well. The footage was sure to make a great promo reel. The producer took everything back to the States and knocked it together. A couple of weeks later, the director of the production company sent the first edit in an email. The subject line of the email read, 'THIS IS FANTASTIC!' I hit the link and started watching. Within seconds I was fuming.

The music was this doomsday crap that was completely wrong. It cut to a series of made-up newspaper articles with headlines describing crocs eating children alive on the streets of Darwin. Then we cut to an over-the-top voiceover.

'Kids of Australia are getting eaten by crocodiles,' a voice bellowed. 'Matt and Jimmy are here to save the day!'

The worst was the interview with Charlene. Every reference to the croc-management program was edited out. It seemed to me that the whole thing had been reduced to a couple of cobbled-together quotes about how much she missed Briony. I felt it was shameful. There was no way my name was being attached to this show, not unless the whole thing was recut. I got on the phone to the producer.

'Hey, Matt,' she said. 'What do you think?'

'I'll be honest,' I said. 'It's not what I had in mind at all. I think we've got a lot of work to do.'

I started off telling her about my disappointment with the interview with Charlene.

'I agree,' she said, with distress in her voice.

She then began opening up about the pressure she'd received on her arrival back to the States from her managers wanting to create a sensationalist piece.

'I am so sorry,' she said. 'I did not want this to be the end result. It doesn't do you or Charlene any justice.'

I felt sorry for the girl and knew it was out of her hands. I hung up the phone and called the director. I told her to can it straight away. She said she couldn't, that I was tied to a contract and didn't have a choice in the matter. I went silent, contemplating my response.

'Yes, I do,' I said. 'I'm out and want nothing to do with you.'

I hung up and that was the end of my short time with Discovery.

I understand that television is a commercial business. You have to produce shows that people want to watch. But I wasn't willing to sell out for the sake of a show I thought was crap. Besides, there is so much real excitement, beauty and danger in the Top End, there isn't any need at all to manipulate the facts. This show for me was about showing the world what happens on a daily basis in this place, not to spin shit for the sake of ratings. The phone call from Nick came about half an hour later.

'What happened?' he said.

'Sorry, mate, but I'm out.'

'Why?'

I listed all the issues I had with the program.

'You can't give up now,' he said.

'Fucking oath I can.'

'But we've worked too hard—'

'Nick,' I said, 'I'm not jeopardising my reputation, my friends, my family, my colleagues just to make bullshit American television.'

I don't know how Nick did it, but the Discovery contract was torn up without any ramifications. I was pretty deflated there for a while and felt bad for Nick. He had invested a lot of time to make the show a reality. There were other people, too – mates who had given up their time to hold a camera or show me how to edit a film or helped in some other way to make the dream come true. I felt like I was letting them down. But if this was what it meant it be on television, I wasn't going to be a part of it.

I needed to get out of Australia to clear my head and work out what was next. I bought myself a ticket to Canada. A season in the snow was just what I needed. A day before I boarded the plane, Nick rang with good news. National Geographic was still interested.

21

Wildfire

The contract with Discovery prevented me from doing a deal with another broadcaster for a year from the date I signed, so I decided to head over to Canada as planned. It would be a good chance for me to get away and form a clear vision of exactly what I wanted the show to look like. Before leaving, I managed to snag a job with Great Slave Helicopters (GSH). The company operated out of Yellowknife, the capital city of the Northwest Territories situated on the northern shore of the Great Slave Lake.

GSH was a great fit for me. Just like Qwest, I hit it off with the other pilots and admin staff straight away. Most of the work involved flying surveyors and scientists out to remote locations in the far north to conduct oil and gas exploration. GSH also offered executive charter flights, air ambulance service, aerial photography, and much more. But there was another service GSH offered, something I hadn't done much of in Canada – fire suppression.

The summer I joined up with GSH was hotter and drier than normal. Although wildfires in the northern regions of Canada are a way of life in the summer months, the towns of the Northwest

Territories and surrounding provinces were bracing for a particularly bad fire season. My experience of aerial firefighting was
limited to slinging a bucket of water from my R44 over a few
spot fires that flared up around Darwin. This was going to be
completely different.

The call came in mid-morning from the Hay River Fire
Department. A lightning strike had started a blaze about 50
kilometres outside of Hay River, a small township on the southern shore of the lake. The fire was not big, but if ignored might
develop into something that could threaten the local community.
The fire department was calling in any available choppers to suppress the blaze. I was one of two chopper pilots who answered
the call. The other chopper pilot – he was a fuckwit and I don't
remember his name so let's call him Dave – worked for a company on the other side of the lake.

I'd only met him once before. He had racked up a lot of hours
fighting fires from his chopper. I got on the radio to Dave. He
made it clear that he planned on calling the shots. He had carried
out reconnaissance on the blaze and told me that although the
fire was small, a stiff southerly was taking it north. It would come
very close to Hay River. Then he outlined his plan for tackling the
blaze. It gave me serious concerns. He wanted to back-burn.

'I'm heading out now with the drip torch to start up a blaze a
mile west of the main fire,' he said.

In opening up a front to the west of the main blaze, Dave was
hoping to draw the fire away from Hay River. This was a proven
method of fire management. A fire produces warmer air that rises
from the heated surface. The cooler, denser air surrounding the
fire rushes in to replace the escaping hot air. The speed at which
the air rushes is proportional to the size of the blaze. Put simply,

the bigger the fire, the stronger the wind created. If Dave could start up a big enough blaze, he could create a vacuum effect and pull the main fire away from the township. Eventually, the two fires would meet. Having burnt up all the available flammable material, the fire would extinguish.

I thought it was a crazy idea. A period of intensely hot and dry weather had left the countryside tinder dry. A controlled burn could quickly become uncontrollable.

'Why don't we just dump a couple of buckets of water on the fire while it's still small?' I asked.

Dave stuck to his guns. He had already got the go-ahead with the fire chief. He told me to get out with the drip torch and help him flare up a blaze.

As it happened, my contribution to the burn was minimal. I was flying one of the company's AS350 Squirrels. I'd connected the drip torch to a length of chain that I locked onto the cargo latch. Once I was airborne, I set a course for Hay River. I had no trouble finding the fire. A huge smoke cloud blotted out the horizon. On approach I could see flames engulfing large spruce trees. The fire was already bigger than I imagined.

I got on the radio to Dave and restated my concerns. Dave was having none of it. He told me to head west and help him get another blaze going. I flew the Squirrel over the main fire and got a visual on Dave's chopper. He was about two kilometres from the main fire and was running his chopper in a straight line parallel to the blaze. I could see his drip torch spitting out burning gel that lit up trees and foliage. He already had a decent blaze going

I flew in behind Dave and started dripping out flames perpendicular to Dave's line. I couldn't believe how quickly the flames took hold. Within moments of dripping out a cupful of gel, entire spruce and pine trees were burning. The southerly breeze picked up in intensity, carrying the flames across the spruce forest at alarming speed. I didn't like it at all. But it was Dave's call. So I pressed on.

I was slinging a 44-gallon drum filled with flammable gel, enough to start a fire that could burn thousands of hectares or set alight a continuous fire front up to 50 kilometres long. I was slowly making my way west, lighting up the forest floor when I felt a sudden upwards lurch. I looked out to see my drip torch disappearing into the forest. I pulled up on the collective. The drip torch exploded on impact, sending up a column of fire that nearly reached the undercarriage of my rising chopper. Either the chain link was faulty or had melted in the heat. Whatever the reason, I was no longer able to help get the blaze going.

I got on the radio and explained the situation to Dave. I told him I was heading back to hook my water bucket onto the sling. Dave didn't respond. He was probably pissed off. But I didn't care. A part of me was pleased I could get on with the business of containing the main fire rather than starting up another one.

I got back to base, picked up a bucket and then dunked it in Great Slave Lake. It took about 30 minutes to get back to the fire with a full bucket of water. What I saw on returning scared the shit out of me. In the half hour I'd been gone, the fire had tripled in size. Fire whirls, like mini-tornados, were dancing high up above the treetops. The fire was generating so much heat that spruce trees at the edge of the fire front were exploding. Dave was nowhere to be seen. I tried to get him on the radio.

'Dave, do you copy?' I asked.

'Yep,' he said, completely calm. 'What's your position?'

'I'm at the edge of our burn,' I said. 'It's time to put a bucket on and put this thing out.'

'Negative,' he said. 'We have to keep stoking it up.'

'It's not going to work!'

'It will,' he said. 'I just have to keep lighting.'

I concluded that Dave was either deluded or a pyromaniac. Either way, I decided I was no longer going to take orders from him.

I slung the bucket over to the edge of the front and hit the release valve. Five hundred litres poured on the fire and evaporated before it hit the ground. At least, that's how it looked from the chopper. I turned the chopper for the lake, filled it up, and carried out another water dump. The effect was minimal. It was time to call in some more help.

I got on the radio to the fire department and told them to send in the water bombers. The chief got on the radio and asked for coordinates. The northwestern edge of the fire was pushing towards an uninhabited stretch along the southern shore of the lake. The northeastern edge, however, had pushed ahead of the original blaze. I was worried that it might bend around and head towards Hay River.

I gave coordinates for the northwestern edge of the fire. Within about 10 minutes, three Canadair CL-215 water bombers came over. One by one, each aircraft dumped 5000 litres of water on the fire. It made no difference. The bombers turned around for the lake to fill up their water tanks. As I watched them turn around, I saw a big plume of smoke come over the top of me. It was the worst possible scenario – the wind changed to an easterly. The fire was now being pushed directly toward the town.

I got back on the radio and warned the fire chief. Hay River was evacuated. The water bombers were redirected to defend the town. Meanwhile, Dave and I were told to cease any fire suppression activities and were placed on standby to assist firefighters setting up a containment line at the western edge of town.

The situation continued to deteriorate. Not only was the wind coming from a different direction, it was stronger. The view from above was incredible. The wind picked up burning embers and hurled them hundreds of metres forward of the main fire front, starting up spot fires.

The chief called us in to defend a small little fishing village to the east of Hay River that was right in the firing line. I went to fill up the bucket while another one of our larger choppers, a 214, unloaded a massive payload of water. As I neared the fire, huge clumps of ash smashed into the window of the chopper. The wind the fire generated was strong – easily in excess of 100 km/h – making it difficult to hover. Because I was downwind of the fire, I was now being bombarded with embers as well as the ash. The heat inside the chopper was nearly unbearable. The hairs on my arms were singed off. I had no choice but to bug out.

I hit the release valve and dumped my bucket of water. It made no impact on the fire. Flames were now flicking over the machine. For a moment, I thought the chopper was alight. There were massive high-wire power lines running along the main road so I turned away from them, giving the Squirrel maximum power. The water bombers and the choppers ceased all fire suppression activities. There was no longer any point – we couldn't see through the smoke with it blackening the day.

At its peak, the fire had a 100-kilometre front and four-kilometre plume of smoke. It looked like a volcano had erupted. All that could be done now was hope and pray that the fire somehow missed the town.

I was absolutely spent. I'd been in the air coming on nine hours. Soon I'd get a call that brought me back to life. I was flying high through the smoke when a firefighter hailed me, saying that his crew was trapped. The fire had crossed the road by this stage and was surrounding them. I raced back and unhooked my bucket in a gravel pit. I hauled arse to their location, finding the firefighters in a perilous position.

A couple waved up at me. They had a hose out pumping water at the burning foliage at the edge of the road. But that would not hold back the fire for long. Flames were leaping 60 feet into the air. Eventually, it would barrel over the top of them.

I set the chopper down not far from the truck. The four firefighters abandoned the truck and sprinted for the chopper. Burning debris was landing in the disc and spraying embers everywhere.

Everyone piled in. I wasted no time getting airborne. As we lifted up, I saw the power lines at the edge of the road melting. I turned the chopper away from the fire as we flew through the black smoke. The boys in the back were coughing up ash and smoke as we cleared off. Below us, the fire truck disappeared in the flames.

* * *

In Canada, helicopter pilots are not allowed to fly more than nine hours a day. It's a strictly enforced rule. As long as that fire was burning, I was given exemption to fly unlimited hours. Over the two horrendous days it took us to get that blaze under control, I clocked up around 25 hours. I was flying back and forth between Great Slave Lake and the fire front, dumping countless buckets of water on the fire. The Squirrel took a hiding. Beneath the chopper's ash-coated fuselage, the blue paint peeled away in the heat.

In the end, we got lucky. No lives were lost in the fire and much of Hay River was saved after a late wind change kept the fire west. But property losses on the outskirts of the town were huge. The damage bill soared into the tens of millions.

When the dust settled, there was a fair bit of arse-kicking. A public inquiry exposed an embarrassing degree of mismanagement on the part of fire officials. Several people lost their jobs for allowing Dave to run rampant with the drip torch and turn a small blaze into a catastrophic wildfire. I fought a few more fires up in the Northwestern Territories that season. But nothing came close to the Hay River debacle. It was some of the most challenging flying I had ever done.

That was the last season I flew in Canada. It was a memorable time of my life but I was ready to return home. I was about to embark on my greatest adventure yet.

22

Wrangler Kicks Off

Nick and I signed a deal with National Geographic in Washington DC for a single season. The show was to be called *Outback Wrangler*. The title was a clear pitch to the American audience. You won't hear too many people using the word 'wrangler' in the Australian outback. In American folklore, a wrangler is the person in charge of livestock or horses on a ranch, kind of like an Australian stockman.

I was prepared to go along with the name of the show provided Nick and I retained editorial control of each episode. My earlier experience dealing with a large American production company had burnt me. There was no way I was going to surrender control of material that had my name on it.

In the end, it was easier than expected. My vision for the show and the sorts of messages that I wanted to get across about conservation and wildlife was completely in sync with the guys across the table. The National Geographic Society has been raising awareness about the natural wonders of the world since it was established in 1888. One of the society's slogans is 'promoting environmental and historical conservation'. This place was going to be a good home for my show.

Other production companies hopped on board, as did Screen Australia. To keep the budget under control, Nat Geo decided to keep the first season down to four one-hour episodes. It turned out that the stuff that really got them across the line was the rough footage Nick and I put together of us clearing nests in Arnhem Land. So I suggested we kick off the series with an episode on egg collecting.

I rang up a few mates and asked if they were interested in coming on board. The Professor and the Wolverine were keen, as were several others. It was an incredible experience. The size of the production was huge. No expense was spared. This was a far cry from the early days of knocking together a short video on a handycam with the help of a mate or a girlfriend. There were cameramen, sound guys, producers, support staff and catering staff.

We named the first episode 'Croc Swarm'. I was thrilled with the quality of the production. It showed the Northern Territory in all its glory. The footage of crocs stalking the collectors and launching at rods and crates was exciting stuff. There was also a hugely suspenseful segment of me standing on the skids of a chopper with pistol drawn as the Professor cleared a nest propped up on floating mat. To make sure the show wasn't too croc heavy, we broke up the episode with a bit of mustering.

Episode two was entitled 'Wild Horse Bust'. This was a show close to my heart, because the subject matter harked back to the initial inspiration that gave rise to the show – wild brumbies. It was a chance to highlight the damage brumbies are doing to the ecosystem while presenting an alternative solution to the problem that didn't involve culling them. The shoot took a couple of days and it proved to be one of the toughest things I have ever done on a cattle station.

Anyone who has worked on a station will tell you that mustering brumbies is tougher than mustering wild cattle or buffalo. Not only are they faster animals, they are also much smarter. But mustering these particular wild horses was harder than normal. The station owner neglected to tell us until after we'd wrapped up filming the episode that the over the previous year he and his boys had shot over 2000 head of wild horses. The surviving horses of that massive cull were understandably wary of people.

In the end, we managed to get 50 of them into the yard and they were vicious. Once we got them in, they bucked and kicked to the point of exhaustion. I got a saddle on one horse. Trying to ride him was a different story. I was thrown off more times than I can remember. It made for a good show, but it hurt like hell. The next two episodes were predominantly focused on crocodiles. To mix things up, we shot one episode in Borneo and the other in the Territory. We edited each episode and then sent them off to National Geographic. They were thrilled, particularly when the show rated well both in Australia and North America. The moment the first episode aired, Nick was fielding calls from Nat Geo executives about another season. I couldn't have been happier. But there was one component of the show's success that I was ill equipped to handle – having a public profile.

* * *

A lot of people are surprised to hear me say that getting the show up and running was not a matter of life and death. I love putting the show together and I'm pleased that *Outback Wrangler* has a great audience. But for me the show has always been about showing people what it's like to live out in the bush, interact with animals and respect the environment. The trade-off for getting a show off the ground is the need to do publicity.

I've never been good at the public speaking thing and have always been on the shy side. Getting a public profile didn't resonate well with me. Immediately after the first season was broadcast, random people started stopping me in the street. I began to notice that blokes in particular would come up and want to challenge me in a bar or when they were on the piss.

On more than one occasion someone bailed me up, shouting, 'You think you're a big tough bull catcher, hey? Let's see how tough you really are!'

This would usually happen in pubs. I'd be quietly having a beer with a mate when suddenly some dickhead full of piss would start carrying on. Before you know it, he's shaping up to take a swing. I've long since learnt to walk away from those situations and I know which pubs to avoid. I find most trouble happens in outback pubs. It's different in the big smoke. City people don't tend to give me any trouble. I put that down to the fact that they've never seen anything like what I do on the show. The worst I get is someone hassling me for a photo or an autograph. And that's fine. I'm grateful that they watch the show. Of all the blow-ups in which I've been involved, one in particular stands out. It was a different sort of altercation to what I'm normally used to. For one thing, it wasn't a bloke.

I met this sheila in a pub up in the Gulf Country. She was sprawled out on a stool, sinking rum, smoking darts and stuffing her face with chips. She had a mouth on her like a truck driver and constantly talked herself up. She was onto me the moment I stepped into the pub.

'I saw your fucking show,' she spat. 'You have no idea how to rope a bull or catch a croc.'

I looked her up and down. I don't want to sound impolite, but she was one big girl.

'You know a bit about that stuff do you?' I asked.

'Fucking oath,' she said. 'I could teach you a thing or two about how to chase down a bull.'

I felt like saying that you'd be stuffed getting off that chair let alone chasing down a bull. But I didn't. I just did my best to ignore her. She spent the next hour levelling every possible criticism at me while tipping a litre of rum down her gullet. All you can do in that situation is laugh.

The show has definitely changed my social habits. I still go out with mates but it's hard to relax when I'm out in public. I have the most fun if I'm just having a BBQ and downing a few beers at a mate's place. Those big messy nights in pubs are no longer an option. The last thing I want is to be that person to get ragged in the media. I get enough heat from authorities just trying to do my job.

Having a public profile is not all bad, though. The time I've spent drumming up interest in the show has had a very positive impact on other businesses that I run. I've had the pleasure of meeting some pretty interesting people, including politicians, prominent businesspeople, professional athletes and Hollywood stars. It seems to be the higher the profile of a celeb the higher the hazard. I learnt that the hard way. Nothing seems to stir up the media quite like an exaggerated story about a well-known Hollywood actor.

23

Gerard Butler

I woke to the sound of my phone beeping. It was a Saturday morning and I was enjoying a sleep-in for once. I stretched across the bedside table, and glanced at the screen. It's never a good sign when you wake up to 35 missed calls and twice as many text messages. Most of the calls were from unknown numbers, so I decided not to look at the others for the time. I turned on the TV to see what was happening in the world, and there it was on every channel around the country. The headlines read 'Gerard Butler injured by cowboy pilot', accompanied by me doing a split-arse turn landing backwards on a sand bar. *Oh shit*, I thought. *This is bad.*

With mounting concern, I scrolled through my text messages, eventually arriving at one sent by my agent. He had texted a YouTube clip of Hollywood star Gerard Butler conducting an interview with American TV host Jimmy Kimmel. I let out a massive groan before I had even watched the clip. This is not what I needed.

I started doing custom tours in 2010. It was an excellent way to supplement my income and they're good fun. They're designed for individuals or small groups who are seeking a proper Territory outback adventure. The custom tours are about taking people out of the humdrum of normal day-to-day living and giving them a glimpse of what I do on a daily basis. We hunt feral animals, go fishing in picturesque inlets, watch crocs and camp in some of the most scenic landscape in the country. They are two- or three-day outback adventure safaris and they have really caught on.

The custom tours are particularly appealing to people who live in a high-stress environment and want to escape and get back to mother nature. A lot of the time these are corporate business-people or high-profile individuals. For celebrities in particular, they relish heading to places inaccessible by road and unreachable by phone. How else do they escape the prying eyes of the media?

Some of the more memorable individuals I've taken out include *Top Gear* presenter Jeremy Clarkson and *Baywatch* star David Hasselhoff. Both men had me in stitches, and gave new meaning to being a fish out of water. But I'd say the most fun I've ever had on one of my trips was with Gerard Butler.

Gerard was out in Australia filming the blockbuster fantasy epic *Gods of Egypt*. He was taking a break from filming and had a few days up his sleeve before he had to get back to Sydney. He was hoping for an off-the-map experience up north, something different from the standard tourist stuff. He made a few phone calls and eventually got onto a mate of mine, who brought him up.

Gerard is a good lad. We got along well – he has a cracking sense of humour, didn't take himself too seriously and there was no ego on show. He was also a keen adventurer. Things did, however, get off to a bit of a shaky start. We flew out to 'the shack' in my R44 for a bit of sightseeing trip. The shack is near Sweets Lagoon and serves as the base for my tourism operation Outback Floatplane Adventures. After lunch, I suggested we go out for a bit of pig hunting. I got out my guns and took the lads through the ropes. I handed Gerard a lever-action .30-30 rifle. I didn't want to patronise him given his alpha male roles in numerous action films, which would have involved extensive handling of firearms. Or so I thought . . .

I handed him the unloaded gun and, as he went to cock it, let's just just say he really cocked it up. He ended up with one of his fingers caught in the action and it began pissing out blood. I had a bit of a laugh and asked if he was okay. I sensed he was a little embarrassed, especially when we had to stick a Band-Aid on to stem the bleeding. Gerard laughed it off well, though, and it became the running joke of the trip. As we were loading the chopper to go hunting, Gerard said he wasn't interested in shooting anything. I wasn't sure if it was for humanitarian reasons or because he was worried he was going to hurt himself again. Either way, he was still eager to get up in the chopper.

We had no problems finding a mob of wild pigs. This part of the country is full of them. If Gerard didn't want to shoot one, it didn't mean he couldn't run one down. I lapped a few around, landed and told the boys to jump out for the chase. They all bolted from the chopper falling straight into the mud, there were limbs flying everywhere as they scurried to their feet to hunt the pigs down. One moment it was Gerard chasing the pig and then it was the pig chasing Gerard. The other fellas were slip-sliding all over the place, falling over their own feet as the pigs escaped. They all came back emptyhanded and puffing but were grinning from ear to ear, and it certainly made for good entertainment for me.

I still needed a pig to feed my pet crocodile Tripod, a big 17-foot fella with only three legs that I keep in a pen out the back of the shack. I ended up shooting a couple of pigs, one for Tripod and one for dinner. We had a great night. We sat outside around a campfire, drinking beers, eating rib bones and trading stories.

The next day I took the lads heli-fishing. I flew us to one of my favourite spots in the Beagle Gulf off Gunn Point. The blue holes there are magic, with pristine coral reef, bright blue water, abundant fish life and turtles everywhere. You can expect to catch big golden trevally, massive cod, snapper and coral trout when you hit a good hole.

It was perfect weather for blue-hole fishing. A gentle breeze that kept us cool was barely strong enough to raise a ripple on the water. Still, you always have to be on your toes as the tides change quick. Gerard cast out for the first time and hooked onto a big trevally right away. He was pulling hard to get it in when out of nowhere a shark sideswiped it, swallowing the fish whole. The force pulled Gerard into the water. The fishing rod was history and Gerard was scrambling up the coral not wanting to meet the same fate as the fish.

Climbing coral at speed is not a forgiving exercise. Gerard was left with some more battle wounds. Poor bloke was starting to look like my 10-year-old nephew after a bike stack. Once we'd bagged a few jack and snapper, we jumped back in the chopper and headed home for lunch. After some fresh fish I dropped the boys on a remote sand island in the middle of the ocean. I flew back to hook up a raft and slung it in the water next to the sand bar. Once I punched it off into the water I proceeded to do a split-arse turn, which is the infamous move that got me in strife.

The move is something I've done time and time again mustering, but I guess it's not something Americans see much of. It's a quick manoeuvre kicking in a heap of pedal while lowering the collective, pointing the tail rotor towards the sky and landing the chopper backwards on the front of the skids. YouTube 'Jimmy Kimmel, Gerard Butler, 2014' to see the clip. Gerard tries to be discreet about the finer details of the trip but something like that is always going to get pumped up in the media.

After one more day sightseeing in the airboat, I took Gerard back to Darwin airport.

'The next time you're in the States,' he said, 'make sure you swing by.'

'Sounds good,' I said.

We shook hands and he boarded his flight. The next time I heard the name Gerard Butler was in the voice messages from the 35 missed calls I woke up to that morning. With my heart in my mouth, I hit the YouTube link my agent had sent. This is an abridged version of Jimmy Kimmel's conversation with Gerard. We pick it up the moment Gerard announces that he was taken on an outback adventure involving crocodiles and boars.

JK: Why were there crocodiles and boars?

GB: This guy is quite a famous adventurer in Australia.

JK: What's his name?

GB: I don't want to say his name.

JK: Oh, okay. Now I really want to hear this story.

GB: There's a lot of stuff I couldn't even put on this video.

JK: Oh, is that right?

GB: This is the tame stuff.

Before the video was shown, Gerard gave a bit more context about the trip. He kicked off with a description of the safety brief I gave him with the low-calibre .30-30 rifle.

> GB: So he gives me this lever-action shotgun, before he even tells me what it's for. I'm thinking, 'I've never used one of these before.' He says, 'Have a hold of that.' So I pull it in and immediately the trigger goes right into my hand . . . I pull it out and the blood is pouring from my hands.

This is what he had to say about the blue hole fishing:

> GB: We did this blue hole fishing. You go in the chopper and you land at the edge of the coral just as the tide has gone out and there are sharks swimming about. And if you catch a fish, you gotta pull it in, in like 10 seconds or the shark is going to take it. We go straight to this blue hole and I end up falling . . . and cut all my leg and blood is pouring out.
> JK: You're bait, at this point.
> GB: I'm bait.

I don't blame Gerard for talking up the trip. In fact, I was honoured he spoke about it in the way he did. His enthusiasm in retelling the story got me excited. I was happy our adventure had left such an impression on him. At this point in the interview, Jimmy Kimmel throws to the clip of me pivoting around the sand bank.

> GB: [Over the video clip] Look at him!
> JK: Oh yeah!

226

GB: I mean, this guy is insane!

JK: This is not a guy you should be hanging around with in general.

GB: This is how we were flying about.

Even though the manoeuvre was nothing I hadn't done before, out of context it did look somewhat reckless. At the end of the video, my mind cast back to a conversation I had with Gerard and the guys in his entourage. I remember telling them that I had no problem with them recording video on their iPhones. If they wanted to show family, friends or colleagues what they got up to, then that was fine by me. It might even generate a bit more work. But I asked that they don't hand over video to the media. Broadcasting unedited clips of outback adventures was a recipe for disaster. Case in point.

I was frustrated because I genuinely take safety very seriously. I run businesses that expose people to potentially dangerous scenarios. There are choppers flying around, floatplanes taking off and airboats whizzing every which way. A lot of the time, I'm taking people up close to crocs. Putting aside the unbearable tragedy of somebody losing their life on one of my tours, the professional and personal consequences for me would be dire. If I was found to have been negligent then I could forget about hanging onto the business, let alone my freedom. I could end up in jail. The outcome would be even bleaker if the accident involved a high-profile celebrity like Gerard Butler.

For all these reasons, safety is always at the front of my mind. When I'm flying in a chopper at 1000 feet, I'm constantly scanning the land beneath me and thinking of the best place to put the chopper down in case of mechanical failure. If I'm flying over water, I'm considering worst-case scenarios and putting together a plan in my head in case of an emergency.

CASA were not impressed, even though the manoeuvre that I performed over that sand bar was nothing I hadn't done as a mustering pilot. It's a standard way of rounding up cattle into a tight group so that they can be herded into the yard. At no point was I in danger of crashing the chopper or endangering the lives of the people on the sand bar.

I got a call from Gerard Butler not long after his appearance on Jimmy Kimmel.

'Hey man,' he said. 'I am so sorry.'

'No worries,' I said.

He suggested I fly over and stay at his California ranch until everything blew over.

'Sounds good, mate,' I said. 'Only this time, no videos.'

24

Animals are the Best Teachers

Most of the time I feel more comfortable and connected with animals than I do with people. I truly believe that animals show us what really matters in life. There are so many ways they protect, inform, comfort, and inspire us. By their very nature, animals live in the moment while us humans tend to worry too much about the future.

Being on the shy side and far from a natural communicator, I've had to train myself to speak on camera and in public. Funnily enough, animals have taught me a lot about being a presenter. For one thing, relying solely on my words is not enough. The tone of a person's voice, facial expression, posture and movements communicate our thoughts, emotions, and intentions, often more so than the words we choose.

I've also learnt a lot about interacting with people. When working with animals, you have to respect their personal space, to never stand above them or intimidate them, and to always be gentle and calm in your approach. If more people interacted with each other in this way, I'm sure the world would be a happier place. I'm certainly still working on it. Animals have also shown me that it's all about time and patience and creating trust and confidence in one another.

But of all the lessons I've learnt from working with animals, following my instincts has been the most important. On this score, no animal has taught me more than crocodiles. Crocs are among the most instinctive creatures in the animal kingdom. They're alert and attentive to each of their senses, responding to cues by trusting their instincts and acting on them. Being able to tap into your own instincts and knowing how to use them constructively is fundamental to working with crocs. The same goes for working with any dangerous animal.

If I didn't have the ability to read the warning signs of animals in the wild, I would probably be dead. Again, I reckon this lesson can be applied to everyday life. When humans rationalise situations, it often leads us to second-guess or ignore what our senses are saying. This puts us at risk of ignoring important signals about events, circumstances, and the people around us.

I've never been very open with my emotions and have always felt uncomfortable discussing things like love or loss. It's not that I haven't felt things strongly. I've just been pretty average at showing and articulating them. Yet I have never struggled to be affectionate with animals; in fact, I'm probably overly affectionate with animals and pretty disengaged with most people. In the peaceful presence of animals, you can get a sense of their affection for your thoughts without having to say anything. No more so than with my best mate and ever loyal dog, Naish.

* * *

My dog Naish is a vivid dreamer. I sometimes come across her barking wildly in her sleep or rolling on her back, eyes tightly shut and legs kicking away like mad. Considering the life Naish has lived, it's not surprising that her dreams are full of adventure.

Naish came into my life as a fiery nine-month-old not long after I returned home from my first year of living in Canada. I was in the middle of a three-month-long instructor's course on the Sunshine Coast. My short-term plan was to become an instructor for my old mentor Graeme Gillies at his chopper school on the Sunshine Coast. Having 'Grade One instructor' on my CV would also help me to get work down the track.

Out of the blue one morning, I got a call from my mate Kenny. Kenny was going through a bad patch. His beautiful American Bulldog, Ice, had recently been bitten by a snake while chasing pigs at Wrotham Park. For Kenny, it was a tragic turn in what had already been a shithouse year. He had recently separated from his wife and they were still divvying up the possessions, one of which was his new pup Maggy, who he'd bought right after Ice's death. Kenny gave me a bell.

'I've got this dog,' he said. 'She's called Maggy and she's an absolute ripper, just like Ice. I'm ringing to see if you want to take her.'

Kenny had moved from Cairns to Townsville and was trying his best to get back on his feet and get his two boys through school. He had no time or place for this new dog, so he had temporarily placed Maggy in the care of an elderly couple who were family friends. The couple lived in a small house on the Sunshine Coast and the energetic dog was causing all sorts of trouble. They needed to get rid of her.

'You're my last hope,' Kenny said. 'Otherwise they'll send her off to the pound.'

I don't know why I agreed to take her on. I was living in an apartment block on the top floor. If the dog was proving a handful in a house, how was she going to go in my apartment? I also didn't really have the time or the money to take on the responsibility of looking after a dog.

But Kenny was a mate who needed help. Besides, I had been looking for a dog like Ice for a long time. Kenny made it sound that Maggy was the perfect pet for someone like me. I figured there was no harm in finding out if he was right. I took down the address of Kenny's family friends and told him I'd pick her up on the weekend.

Back then, I was driving a red 1967 two-door Camaro. It was left-hand drive. Although it cost a bit to run, it was a tough little car, nothing at all like the cars they make these days. I was going to get a 1966 Fastback Mustang until a mate I flew with in Canada said he had a Camaro back in Australia that he wanted to sell. I bought it for a song.

I pulled up at the address Kenny had given me and rang the doorbell. From inside, I could hear the dog going crazy. She was barking her head off. An old man opened the door, relief flooding across his face when I told I'd come to pick up the dog. He told that me they'd had her for about three months. In that time, she hadn't left a thing unchewed – from electrical sockets, to chairs and shoes.

I went inside to get the dog. She had a leash on and was going mental. I managed to grab hold of her and gently tugged on her leash, trying to get her to calm down. When that didn't work, I wrenched her towards me. I took her under my arm and introduced myself. She barked a few times, licked my face and then tried to run off again.

'Good luck,' said the old man, quickly closing the door behind me.

With great difficulty, I managed to open up the passenger door to the Camaro and shove her in. She went wild inside the car, barking madly while leaping from seat to seat, smashing into each door. I raced around and opened up the driver's door, she barrelled out through my legs. I turned and made a lunge for her, managing to grab hold of the leash. *Maybe this wasn't such a great idea*, I thought.

'Come here!' I shouted.

I pulled her towards me, picked her up and threw her into the car. She tried to crawl over me again, but I managed to pull the car door shut before she had a chance to leap out.

'Sit down!' I said sternly, forcing her into the front passenger seat. I held her down for a couple of seconds, hoping she would calm down. Every time I let go, she would spring to life, jumping all over me and drooling everywhere. Eventually, after about 10 minutes, her energy started to sap.

'All right,' I said. 'We've got a bit of a drive ahead of us.'

The drive from the Sunshine Coast to the Gold Coast takes a little over two hours. I was trying to convince myself that it would all be over quickly.

Sure enough, it started out okay. Maggy made a lot of noise, but she kept relatively still. The roar of the engine was scaring her. I don't think she had heard anything like that before. I could see she was nervous and a little out of her comfort zone, but I wasn't expecting her next move.

The moment we hit the Sunshine Motorway, the drive became

a nightmare. Maggy nearly died. She leapt out the window, trying to escape. I managed to grab hold of her tail and hung on for dear life. If the force of hitting the road at speed didn't kill her, then the truck behind me would have cleaned her up. I tried to wrench her back inside, but this dog was determined to escape. I had to hang on to her tail for a few minutes until I finally came onto an exit ramp.

I took the exit and found a quiet little backstreet. I pulled the car over, wrenched Maggy back from the window and gave her a hard talking-to. She whimpered, leapt into the back and cowered into the seat. I took the opportunity to wind up the window before turning around to look at my new dog. She was scared and confused. I felt sorry for her, but I needed to take the opportunity to teach her that it's not acceptable to jump out onto the motorway.

I've trained many dogs in the past and it's important to teach discipline and respect without breaking their spirit. A dog without respect is impossible to have a relationship with. I had an idea up my sleeve that would put her at ease and make her relax during the road trip in the noisy car. The next stop was the pie shop.

With Maggy devouring three steak and kidney pies, I pulled out from the kerb, swung the Camaro around and got back onto the motorway. Maggy was one happy pup. She left a terrible mess, but there's no better way to a dog's heart than with a killer feed.

Once we got back to my place I was looking at this dog thinking that there is no way in hell I was having a dog named Maggy. Who the hell calls a dog that anyway? That night, all sorts of names were running through my head. I considered Milo, Molly, Mogs and Mischief, but none of them had a ring to it. Then in popped Marley. I liked the sound of that and tested it out on Maggy.

For the next month, Maggy turned to Marley and she didn't know any different. That was until I went to the video store to get out a movie and there was Owen Wilson and Jennifer Aniston cuddling on the front of a DVD with a Golden Retriever. The film was titled *Marley and Me*.

'Ah, fuck it!' I blurted out.

Maggy could no longer be Marley. So what was it going to be? This poor dog was going to get very confused before too long. The brainstorming started again and still nothing stuck. A few weeks later I was out on my stand-up paddleboard with Maggy. A few mates were on their paddleboards and we were talking about potential names. I looked down at the dog in question and in front of her was the brand of the board. The brand was Naish.

'Naish,' I said.

It had a ring to it and suited the big eyes peering back at me.

'Naish,' I said again and my dog started wagging her tail. There was a smile on her face, too. Bingo! That was it. My not-so-new dog's name would be Naish.

The early days living in my apartment were pretty tricky given there was a rule prohibiting dogs being inside. When we arrived home each night I'd pull out a huge duffel bag. I'd pack Naish in, gently lifting her inside the bag. She didn't put up any resistance, as if sensing she had to hide. I'd slug the duffel bag over my shoulder, saying g'day to neighbours who waved back, none the wiser. The landlords called me one day enquiring as to whether I had a dog.

'Are you keeping a dog in your room?' they asked.

'No,' I said.

'Where do you keep your dog?'

'At the helicopter school.'

I doubt he believed me but he had no way of proving his suspicion. In the end, I had to buy a house on the Sunshine Coast, just so I had somewhere to put my dog. We stayed in the house on the Sunshine Coast for a couple of months. After I got my instructor's rating it was back to the life of a line pilot. If I had any concerns about letting Naish loose on a cattle station, I shouldn't have. She took to her new surrounds like a fish to water. She loved the open spaces and was always a favourite with ringers and station hands, no matter where we went.

Naish still took a lot of hardcore training before she was obedient. But bloody hell, it was worth it. She became, and still is, the most affable dog I've ever come across. Not only was she good fun and great company, but she never complained when we had to sleep in a swag, stay away from home, eat tinned tuna or get grubby. Best of all, she loved fishing. That's why Naish has always been the main lady in my life. I have shared the best times of my life with Naish but we've certainly had some hairy moments, too.

I was on my way to the Sunshine Coast once and had to stop off at a station on the way to muster some bullocks. They were playing hardball to get out of the jungle. I brought Naish along for the ride in the chopper. Just as I came down on one of these bullocks, a dirty old black and white boar ran out of the long grass directly in front of the chopper. Without hesitation, Naish launched out of the chopper and chased after the boar into the thick jungle. This was bad. Naish had no protection and the pig had the biggest set of hooks I'd ever seen.

I landed the chopper as quick as I could, grabbed my .357

from under the seat and took off in the same direction. I could hear the commotion as I approached. I entered into the clearing and saw Naish getting flung around but she wasn't letting loose. A lot of damage had already been done and Naish was red all over. As I got closer, the pig flung Naish 10 feet into the air and turned for me.

The pig came at me at full force. There was no time to waste. Naish was bleeding to death and the pig wasn't taking any prisoners. I unleashed a flurry of bullets into the boar's skull. The pig was dead before he hit the ground.

I ran to Naish, scooping her up and running as fast as I could back to the chopper. She had deep holes all over her body – in her chest, throat, chin and legs. It was like someone had hacked at her with an axe. I got rags and gaffer tape to wrap her up and stop the bleeding. She looked like a silver mummy once I was done. There was no vet nearby and I needed to remain out at the station for another night. I did some makeshift stitching on my dog that night. She was very well behaved and let me sew up the big gashes. The bleeding had stopped and she had stabilised overnight but still needed proper treatment. I took her to the vet as soon as we got to town and they said she was lucky to be alive.

This isn't the only sticky situation that Naish has got herself into over the years. She has nearly overheated chasing down big bullocks; almost drowned in swamps because she can't swim; come close to being eaten by a crocodile during a relocation; was bitten by a snake because she got too inquisitive; had her paw chomped on by a mud crab; and was chased in the shallows by a shark while I was fishing. Somehow, she has managed to live through it all.

It has been nine years since I picked Naish up from the house in the Sunshine Coast. Taking her on was one of the best decisions of my life. She's one special dog with a pretty incredible spirit. I'm hoping to get some little Naish's out of her soon. There needs to be more like her in the world. The hard part will be finding her a worthy suitor!

25

Little Legend

My beautiful daughter Brooke came into the world in 2007. Brooke's mum Cristie is a fantastic mother and I feel very lucky to have such a great relationship with both Cristie her partner Trent. Trent has been an incredible father figure to Brooke since she was born. Cristie and Trent have raised Brooke and her two younger sisters on a cattle station in northern Queensland.

If there's one thing Brooke has inherited from me, it's her love of animals. She's got a menagerie of green frogs scattered around the pot plants at her house. She absolutely adores her pet pigs Speckles, Pepper and Charger, and rides her horse Cowboy religiously. She loves showing her yabbies Danielle from Danger Lagoon and Earl from Earl's Lagoon to her friends and family.

If I had to imagine the life I would want for my daughter it is the exact life she is living now. Brooke is away from the toxicity of city life. She does school of the air, the generic term for correspondence learning for kids growing up in remote places. She plays outdoors with her sisters and rides her horses. Cristie and

Trent have created a great family life, one I feel very lucky to be a part of. I cherish the relationship that Brooke and I have and we've had some great adventures together over the years.

Brooke is an inquisitive and wholehearted girl with a contagious giggle and enthusiasm for everything around her.

One of my favourite memories with Brooke harks back to when she was a little four-year-old. I took her for a walk down the river with Naish. We were wandering along laughing and chatting when Naish decided to bolt off into the bushes. Brooke and I kept walking until we heard loud squealing and grunting noises. Brooke gasped and looked up at me with fear in her eyes. I picked her up and we started running through the scrub towards the noise.

Naish had found herself a big pig and was getting swung around like a rag doll. It wasn't pretty. Brooke couldn't comprehend what she was seeing. I had to act quickly. I stuck Brooke in a tree and told her to stay there while I went to help Naish. The situation was complicated by the fact that I didn't have a gun or knife. Somehow I had to get Naish off the pig.

I managed to grab hold of the pig and pull him down hard. Once I had the pig pinned down under my knee, I took hold of Naish with one hand. She was bleeding and the big pig was wound up and surely ready to charge. I needed to work out a way of getting away with my dog without either of us being ripped apart by that pig's tusks. It was a dire situation and it was about to get a whole lot worse.

'Excuse me, Matt,' came a voice from behind. 'What's wrong with the pig's ear?'

I turned around, clapping eyes on Brooke standing there looking puzzled. There wasn't enough time to tell her to head back up the

240

tree. The pig was bucking like mad and beginning to wriggle free.

'Okay, Brookey,' I said, keeping my voice calm. 'Here's the plan. I'm going to pick you up and we're going to go for a bit of a run. Are you ready?'

'Yep!' said Brooke with a giggle. She loves an adventure.

Firmly clasping Naish under one arm, I grabbed Brooke in the other and bolted out of the bushes. With the pig hot on my heels, I raced back down the path and over the fence. The whole time Brooke was laughing her head off. Cristie and Trent would have hung me alive if they knew the extent of the situation. When we got home, Brooke started telling her grandiose story to her mum while I did my best to play parts of it down.

* * *

To get out to the station where Brooke lives is a six-hour drive from Cairns – so not the most accessible place in the world. Around the time Brooke was turning six, I borrowed my mate's chopper and flew to the station from Cairns to spend time with her. Upon arrival, an excited Brooke greeted me and took me around the side of the house to show me something. Brooke leaned down into a pipe and pulled out a three-foot python with a big grin on her face.

'Meet my new pet,' she said, smiling ear to ear. Each time I see Brooke her love and fascination with animals seems to grow and grow.

The next day we took the chopper fishing down the river to see if we could land ourselves some big barra. Brooke and her sisters went off for a walk. A couple of minutes later, Brooke came running back to tell me they'd found a big snake in the waterhole where they were trying to swim. So we went to investigate.

Sure enough, there was huge body coiled up under a log near the water. My first instinct was that it was a brown snake, certainly not an animal to treat lightly. I couldn't see the full body so I told the girls to stand back and grabbed him by the tail. I pulled it out and saw that it was a very large water python.

'All good,' I said. 'It's not a venomous one.'

'Does that mean I can hold it now?' asked Brooke.

I handed the 10-foot snake over to Brooke who wrapped it around herself cuddling it like a teddy and walked off into the bushes to let it go.

A more recent adventure with Brooke was to Australia Zoo, the 100-acre zoo on the Sunshine Coast. It was an absolute playground for both of us. Brooke developed an instant fascination with the water dragons that were running around the grounds. She was dead set on chasing one down to hold. I couldn't interest her in any other attraction or animal. Most of the day was spent following them around in the heat until I finally managed to get one in my arms. I handed it to her and it was like all her Christmases had come at once.

We were able to visit the other animals and got pictures with the koalas and seals. When we came across the zoo's big eagle, Brooke was told she was allowed to hold it. After I explained that they're not easy birds to handle, she was happy to move on.

Every time we catch up over the phone Brooke has yet another wildlife story. The last time we spoke I got a blow-by-blow description of a kookaburra hunting a frog.

'The kookaburra was banging the frog on the post really, really hard,' she said. 'But it's all part of the circle of life!'

It always makes me laugh to hear how much she loves nature and animals. At her age, I was exactly the same. What really cracked me up, though, was when I spoke to her just after her ninth birthday.

'Out of all the animals, what is your favourite?' I asked.

She only needed a second before answering, 'Well, it has to be a crocodile, of course!'

26

How I Like to Live

It's pretty ironic that, after all the years of working with crocodiles and flying choppers, the worst injury I've ever suffered was on holiday in South Australia a few years back. Mum was living in Hahndorf, a beautiful little town 30 minutes' drive east of Adelaide. I flew in from Darwin and caught a bus to Mum's place. I arrived in the early afternoon.

The old girl was still at work so I headed to the stables at the back of her place to say hello to the horses. One of the horses was Chas, a beautiful bay gelding I rode growing up. Chas's ears pricked up when I walked into the stable. I figured once I'd been for a ride Mum would be home.

I threw the saddle on, strapped him up and set off. He was pulling hard at the reins the moment I was in the saddle so I trotted him out to a back paddock and let him loose. After a good run up and down the valleys, I turned us back for home. That was when we ran into trouble.

While crossing a bitumen road, Chas's front legs slipped away. He fell sideways and I went with him, taking the brunt of the impact along the lower right side of my body. Chas was a big, powerful horse and his whole weight rolled on top of me. It didn't hurt nearly as much as I anticipated, but I cringed at the sickening sound of breaking bones. I was devastated for my old horse. The sound I heard could only mean he had broken a leg.

To my astonishment, Chas leapt up and showed no sign of injury. I pulled myself up, taking a quick step towards him when my right leg gave way and I collapsed in a heap. I looked down, my mind taking a couple of seconds to register what I was seeing. My right pant leg was stained cherry red and my right foot was bent the wrong way. Chas wasn't hanging around. He bolted away, disappearing behind a hill. I was left sprawled out across the bitumen. I managed to get upright and hopped on my good leg across the road. Each time I landed, the force jolted through my body and made me wince in agony.

Once off the road, I lowered myself to the ground and carefully hitched my pants to reveal the extent of the injury. It looked like a compound fracture – my tibia had broken through the skin and the wound was haemorrhaging. My foot was also badly injured and was sticking out at a right angle.

Initially, the pain was manageable, but it was a different story when I tried to move. One minute I wanted to spew, the next I was seeing stars. I needed a tourniquet. The best I could come up with was my belt. I fumbled it off my trousers and tied it around the point where the bone stuck out of my leg. I looked around for a stick or a branch to use as a splint.

It was at that point I heard the first car. I whipped my head around and saw a sedan whiz past. I needed to get to higher ground so the driver of the next car saw me. Back first, I dragged myself along the side of the road using my arms to lever my arse off the ground. I managed to move about 40 metres in 10 minutes. I shimmied under a gum tree and lent against the trunk. I was still slightly lower than the road, but it was the best I could do.

The day was getting seriously hot, easily nudging 40 degrees. My blood was drawing the flies and the pain was getting steadily worse. After about an hour of being under the tree, another car came past. I shouted at the top of my voice and waved my arms, but the driver kept going. The same thing happened 10 minutes later and another 10 minutes after that. Nobody could see me.

After the last car drove past, I was beginning to think that my best hope was Chas. Presumably, he would head back home. When Mum saw him saddled up on the day I was due to arrive, she would put two and two together. I took another deep breath, steeling myself against the ever-worsening pain. The lower right side of my body felt like it was on fire. But I knew I couldn't panic. That was a sure way of making a bad situation much worse. Luckily, I didn't have that much longer to wait. An old woman who lived on the farm next to where I was sitting, had heard me calling out for help. She came down to inspect what was happening.

'Hello?' she said, in a heavy German accent

'I *need* water,' I said, moving my arm to my mouth to signal what I meant.

She nodded and quickly walked off. She returned a few minutes later with a full bottle of water.

'Thank you,' I said, relieved that she had understood my meaning.

All I wanted was to down as much water as possible. The lady had other ideas. She'd seen my leg more closely and started shaking her head. She then said something in German, unscrewed the cap of the bottle and filled it with water, handing me a cap of water. I swallowed it in one gulp but she wouldn't give me the whole bottle. I was frustrated and had no idea, at that point, why she didn't give me the bottle.

After two more capfuls of water, she screwed the cap onto the bottle and said something with an apologetic look on her face. I was absolutely parched. I pleaded with her to give me more. If she didn't understand the words, she would have understood the look on my face. The woman shrugged and sat down alongside me. It turned out she had some medical knowledge. After taking one look at my leg, she correctly concluded that I would need surgery. The last thing you want to do before surgery is load up on water.

It took 20 minutes for the ambulance to turn up. By that point, I was in a lot of pain. I swore my head off when I was lifted onto the gurney. They wheeled me into the ambulance and then one of the ambos injected me with some strong painkillers. I can't remember much from that point. They took me to the hospital and sent me straight into the operating theatre.

The surgeon told me the next day that Chas had done a proper job on my leg. I had a hairline fracture to my foot, five shattered toes, a broken ankle, broken tibia and broken fibula. Sitting in that hospital bed, waiting for the cast to properly set, I started to take stock. When I tallied up the injuries I had suffered in my life, I realised I had come out extremely well. The busted leg in Hahndorf was a reminder of how lucky I'd been.

* * *

For me, catching crocs, flying choppers, collecting croc eggs and mustering animals is like driving a car at night. You can observe the speed limits, stop at the red lights and make sure your head-lights are switched on. But that doesn't mean a truck isn't going to come out and sideswipe you. No matter what you do, some-times things go wrong. There's no way of safeguarding against every possible disaster or misfortune.

We all have the choice in life of whether we want to live inside our comfort zone or take risks. Before the launch of the first season of *Outback Wrangler*, right when I started to get some traction in the mainstream media, television host Mike Munro asked me a question about the risks involved in what I do.

'Do you think about how Steve Irwin ended up?' Mike asked.

'Yeah, I do,' I said. 'That's part of working with wildlife.'

'And (you're) prepared for that?'

'Yep, definitely.'

Some people were surprised to hear me answer that way, but it's not like I have a death wish. I just believe in taking life head on.

The way I see it, life is tough and challenging. Sometimes we feel happy and sometimes we feel sad. The reality is that we all die one day so we may as well give it a good old crack. For me, the only way to do that is to fill it with adventure, learn new things, share ideas, take risks, make mistakes, have pride in what I do, give to others, be kind, work hard and operate outside of my comfort zone. If I can throw in the towel at the end of it all knowing I've done this, then I'll be stoked.

ABOUT THE CO-AUTHOR

Tom Trumble has worked in journalism, policy development and book retailing. He graduated with honours in history, and has also studied music and journalism. He is the author of *Unholy Pilgrims* (2011), *Rescue at 2100 Hours* (2013) and *Tomorrow We Escape* (2014), all published by Penguin Random House. He lives in Melbourne.